Connecting Paradigms:
A Trauma-Informed & Neurobiological Framework for Motivational Interviewing Implementation

Matthew S. Bennett

Copyright © 2017 by Matthew S Bennett

All rights reserved.

First Printing, 2017

Bennett Innovation Group, L3C
Denver, Colorado

www.connectingparadigms.org

Books may be purchased in quantity and/or special sales by contacting the publisher, by email at matt@BIGL3C.org.

ISBN: 9781521800850

To all the clients I have worked with throughout my career. You have been my greatest teachers.

CONTENTS

	Acknowledgments	1
	Introduction	3
1	The Trauma-Informed Paradigm	12
2	Trauma and Human Development	22
3	The Brain and Trauma	34
4	Basics of Motivational Interviewing	52
5	The Mind and Stages of Change	62
6	MI Process Engage	81
7	Trust and Safety	97
8	MI Process Focus	111
9	Mindfulness	125
10	MI Process Evoke	138
11	Mindsight	152
12	MI Process Plan	165
13	Post-traumatic Growth	178
	Conclusion	188
	Bibliography	192
	Index	198

ACKNOWLEDGMENTS

The process of writing and editing Connecting Paradigms was a labor of love and I never could have completed it without the incredible support and help of my friends and family.

Sarah Bennett is my wonderful wife and first editor of this book. I made a deal with her that I would clean the house every week if she spent a good part of her Saturdays editing my first draft. Not only did Sarah do a fantastic job editing, her support also kept me focused and motivated every step of the way. I am lucky to be married to my best friend whose love has allowed me to explore my passion and turn it into a career.

I also thank my good friend, trauma-informed champion, and Motivational Interviewing guru Russha Montag Knauer. Russha served as the second editor and gave up so much of her time to help with the Connecting Paradigms project. This book was in great part inspired by the conversations Russha and I have shared over the years. Her brilliance and passion contributed greatly to this book.

My mother Nancy Leffler was a constant and relentless editor at every stage of development. As a former teacher, her attention to detail was remarkable and her cheerleading priceless! I could not have done it without you mom.

I was lucky enough to find a great final editor in Kathy Nida. Having a basic understanding of trauma-informed schools rendered her the perfect person to polish and finalize the book. I could not have asked for a better partner.

I would also like to thank my former teammates at the Coldspring Center. I wrote Connecting Paradigms when I was the Coldspring Center's Chief Innovation Officer. They generously allowed me to utilize the hundreds of pages of content that we had created over the years. Bettina Harmon, Kate Leos, Olga Vera, Brooke Bender, and Robert George, I count myself incredibly fortunate for having had the opportunity to work with each one of you.

My journey to writing Connecting Paradigms was guided by all the amazing mentors and brilliant thinkers I have met along the way. Dr. Jerry Yager introduced me to the trauma-informed paradigm in 2005 and mentored me as an eager new student to becoming a teacher myself. It is hard for me to imagine what my life and career would look like had I not had the opportunity and great fortune to work with Jerry.

Dr. Deborah Borne, Holly Hanson, Karen Mooney, and Dr. Barbara DiPietro (and her colleagues past and present at the National Health Care for the Homeless Council) also have played important roles as mentors and teachers who have taught me so much and pushed me to realize my Potential as a writer and trainer. Your love and support over the years is why I had the confidence to write Connecting Paradigms.

Finally, I want to thank all those that have supported my work as a blogger and trainer. For your dedication to the service of your community, you are my inspiration. Thank you for supporting my work and never giving up on those that need your love and expertise.

INTRODUCTION
JOURNEY TO THE PARADIGMS

Connecting Paradigms is written to fill a void in the social-work, psychology, educational, and public-health literature. It is a void that I felt all too powerfully when I left the halls of academia and entered the helping professions. This void, stated simply, is that I had no idea why my clients struggled the way they did or what my clients needed from me as a counselor, educator, case manager, or therapist to help them change behaviors that kept them trapped in cycles of violence, addiction, and extreme poverty. *Connecting Paradigms* ambitiously seeks a comprehensive answer to the who, what, and how of helping others live the best life possible.

Looking back, I do not see my education as a waste of time and money. Instead, it was representative of the lack of science we had at the time to understand the work of helping others. I viscerally felt this void when I sat down with my first client.

Fresh out of undergrad with a degree in human services, I was hired by a residential juvenile justice facility. Most of my clients were from the Southside of Indianapolis, Indiana. During the crack epidemic of the mid-1990s, two Chicago gangs, the Vice Lords and Gangster Disciples, were battling over the territory, making the Southside of Indianapolis one of the most dangerous neighborhoods in the entire country. It was into this dark and troubling environment that I walked, with all the excitement and passion that had been building in me for years as a student. I was finally going to help people change their lives and be a catalyst for change in the larger community in which I worked.

I set out with the dream of becoming the next great existential therapist. In the vein of Rollo May, I was going to spend my life's work helping people resolve deep existential crises, helping a new and stronger person emerge from these defining life moments. Then my supervisor put a stack of files in front of me detailing the lives of the children I would be working with and their families. I still remember the thud those files made; the echo of that thud continues to affect my life and career.

My clients were teenagers fighting a gang war, living in impoverished and broken homes, often with a father in prison and a mother struggling with addiction. They went to an underfunded school where students were surviving more than learning. These children lived in a community where they were viewed as thugs, drug dealers, murderers, and criminals before they committed their first crime. By age 16, they had experienced or participated in murder, robbery, drug abuse and distribution, sexual assault, and physical and emotional abuse, and they saw little hope that life would get better.

In other words, in the first hours of my career, I had to reevaluate both my conception of my career focus and my worldview. I realized that I had no clue where to start or even what my clients and their families needed to redirect their lives away from the trauma and tragedy that dominated their worlds. How could I counteract years of poverty, trauma, family and community dynamics, and hopelessness? At 21 years old, I was given the responsibility by my employer and the criminal justice system to help these children accomplish what seemed increasingly like an impossible feat.

I remember feeling like a car tire with a puncture hole as my excitement and passion left my body and mind. No one in my undergraduate work had explained how difficult my chosen career path would be once I was out in the world. Psychology is a beautiful thing to read about in books. I could spend hours lost in the works of Carl Jung or Aaron Beck, contemplating the nature of human consciousness and the role of the unconscious. In contrast, the work I was doing was about helping children survive in the very communities they called home, the same communities that traumatized and victimized them. Dedicating my life to helping others sounded great, but being asked to help these children given my lack of skills and even fewer resources was overwhelming.

My only consolation was that I was starting my master's program in counseling psychology; surely, I would learn the secrets of psychology and would be able to do something for these young clients. I approached my graduate work with vigor and enthusiasm, looking for anything I could take back into my work. I saw every book, report, or assignment as an opportunity to dig as deep as I could for answers as to how I could help the children and families I worked with heal and thrive.

There was a real life-or-death feeling to this search. I realized that what I was doing was not having the results my clients needed, and discharging them back into a war zone just set them up for imprisonment, pain, and even death. This digging led me from psychology to Eastern mysticism to quantum physics and down many other related and unrelated rabbit holes of modern and traditional wisdom.

While this manic chase for knowledge and skills challenged my thinking and opened new possibilities for healing, I found little that I could then apply to my actual work with my clients. I was stumbling in the dark, picking up stones. I had collected some beautiful nuggets of knowledge, but I found no light to guide my thinking or work.

As I completed my graduate degree in psychology, I had a brain full of information but still little understanding of my clients' struggles. What could I do to help them free themselves from their pain or change behaviors that were getting their peers killed on the streets? About the only thing I could say with total confidence was that I loved the work and found great joy and learning from my interactions with clients. This passion kept my search for knowledge burning strong long after I received my graduate degree in counseling psychology.

In the three years it took to get my master's degree, I had found a new related love: leadership and systems theory. It did not take me long to realize the total ineffectiveness of my clinical work in a system that threw my young clients back into communities and families struggling with violence, poverty, and addiction. In the summer of 2000, I moved from central Indiana to Denver, Colorado, and while I continued working with children and their families, I started a master's degree in business administration in healthcare in search of larger system answers.

This degree and a few promotions shifted my focus from direct clinical work to creating and managing clinical staff and programming. I was now responsible for creating programmatic healing experiences for clients and ensuring I had the best team possible doing the work. While this shift in focus presented a different set of tasks and challenges, my inability to fully conceptualize the psychological and social needs of the clients in my programs still limited my ability to help them reach the outcomes we wanted for them.

By 2003, I had worked as a case manager, counselor, and therapist, while having run housing, special education, residential, after-school, in-home therapy, substance abuse, and community-based programming. I had two master's degrees and thousands of hours of experience, and I still felt like I was crawling around a dark cave looking for a light to help illuminate my thinking and work.

One day, my then boss and now friend and mentor Dr. Jerry Yager sat me down in supervision and presented the Adverse Childhood Experience (ACE) Study to me. For the first time, I learned about how past pain and suffering influenced client behavior and psychological functioning well after the event had ended. Not only did the ACE Study provide a model for understanding behavior when coupled with the evolving field of neurobiology, but it also provided a scientific model for designing programs and delivering therapeutic services. Even in his brief introduction, there was finally a spark of light in the dark cave.

For the first time, I started to see a path forward out of the darkness, but my excitement was mixed with sadness and anxiety. My first reaction to trauma research was to see the faces of all those clients I had worked with over the years. I felt extreme sadness that my lack of understanding limited my ability to help them in the way I so desperately wanted.

In the next moment, I thought about all the clients and staff that were currently in the programs I was leading. As I considered this new paradigm, I saw areas of improvement for our program where we could make even minor changes that could result in big differences. Starting to formulate what they did need from us, I realized that we were not currently funded or structured in a way that could truly meet their needs.

Even with the ever-present lack of adequate funding, I had a path forward and found ways to evolve to be more in line with the trauma research. My reading and research shifted to everything I could find on trauma, which at the time was not much. However, there was a growing body of literature coming out on neurobiology, the science of the brain and nervous system.

The 1990s were the "Decade of the Brain." By the early 2000s, this massive amount of research was hitting bookshelves and starting a revolution in how we understand ourselves as human beings. The more I read about the brain, the more I realized what support and resources my clients needed to live a fulfilled life. While it did not decrease the challenge of my work, it provided a scientific foundation to work from, something that I lacked up to this point.

As I was building this new knowledge base on what has become known as trauma-informed care, I was asked to do some training for HIV providers on basic helping skills that they could use with their clients and patients. This opportunity gave me a chance to start to share some of my insights on trauma and the brain. The first several trainings were well-received, and I was asked to do several more, eventually creating a series of trainings.

Much of the work in HIV entails helping clients change behaviors. Whether it is improving sexual health, addressing substance-use concerns, or adhering to medical treatment, the case managers and medical providers I trained were always talking about behavioral change. What I heard from these helpers was that their clients and patients were struggling to make healthier choices even when confronted with overwhelming evidence that a change was needed.

While the research on the brain provided a context for understanding the behavioral and psychological struggles of clients, I needed another set of tools to assist those I trained in their discussions around difficult changes. Luckily, it did not take me long to come across Motivational Interviewing (MI). MI provided me with some much-needed tools in my journey to helping clients heal and to maximize opportunities for behavioral change.

As I conducted more trainings in trauma, neurobiology, and MI, I found a natural fit philosophically between the science of neurobiology, the philosophy of trauma-informed care, and the practical tools of MI. In other words, I now had a scientific foundation in which to ground my work and the skills to help clients both heal and achieve critical changes in behavior.

The void I felt so strongly earlier in my career was starting to get filled. While I still had tons of room for growth and mastery on all these evolving paradigms, I was no longer stumbling around in the dark. Individually, trauma, neurobiology, and MI are powerful and take practice and coaching to master or fully grasp. Together, I have found that they complement each other and lead to better programmatic and clinical outcomes.

Connecting Paradigms is the book I wish someone would have handed me before my supervisor dropped that stack of files on my desk on the first day of my helping career. The goal is to bring these powerful concepts together in a way that can help direct the conceptualization and delivery of services in social work, health care, psychology, education, and other related fields. I hope that you gain as much as I have by this exploration!

LANGUAGE OF CONNECTING PARADIGMS

The information presented throughout this book can be applied in different settings and by a diverse range of professionals who work with people trying to make positive life changes and overcome past suffering and trauma. Each setting has its unique language and terminology. This book uses language that strives to be universal so that it may be applicable in most contexts.

Connecting Paradigms uses the word "client" to describe a person who is seeking assistance from an organization, system, school, or individual. The word "client" may also represent patients in a healthcare setting, students in school settings, or participants in social-service programs. The term "helper" is used to describe those who interact with clients. "Helper" can vary from a physician to a cafeteria worker to a psychologist. Everyone who interacts with clients plays a critical role in creating a nurturing environment that promotes positive change and well-being.

Next is a brief introduction to each paradigm that we will explore in detail throughout this book.

TRAUMA-INFORMED PARADIGM

Connecting Paradigms begins by looking at the evolving science concerning the effects of stress and trauma on human development, psychological and cognitive functioning, and behavior. These scientific advancements call into question many of the traditional theories that have guided psychology, public policy, education, and health care. This book utilizes the trauma-informed paradigm as a lens that allows a deeper and more thorough understanding of how we help clients heal and make critical behavioral changes.

In the future, hopefully, most aspects of health care, education, social services, and policy will be based on the research presented throughout this book. Right now, we are in a crucial transitional stage and can aid this transformation by bringing our services, operations, and funding structures in line with trauma research. This paradigm challenges helping professionals to take a critical look at our roles, services, and organization to make necessary changes, giving clients the maximum benefit of the trauma-informed paradigm.

Any new paradigm needs leaders and champions to realize its true potential on a societal level. *Connecting Paradigms* will provide you with the science behind the trauma paradigm. My challenge to you is to think of yourself as a leader in the movement. Please share this information with co-workers, your friends and family, your child's principal, and government officials. We will always be challenged to integrate the trauma-informed paradigm with our clients as long as we live in communities that do not understand those we are trying to help.

MOTIVATIONAL INTERVIEWING

It is important to take a moment to give credit where credit is due. William Miller and Stephen Rollnick are the founders of Motivational Interviewing (abbreviated as MI throughout the book) and have spent the last several decades developing it into the intervention presented here. In 2012, they published the third edition of their book *Motivational Interviewing*. The new edition has taken some great leaps from past editions and is referenced throughout this book. The goal of this book is to leave the reader with a complete understanding and the confidence to apply MI while using neurobiology and trauma-informed approaches to add valuable new insights beyond previous explorations of this approach.

As you move toward mastering MI, Miller and Rollnick's book will be useful in reinforcing the content in this book. You can also find a variety of books on using MI with specific populations and in specific settings. I have done my best to cite and give credit at every opportunity to Miller and Rollnick, but even this probably falls short of the credit deserved. It is my humble hope that this book furthers the work of two men who deserve tremendous respect for their contribution to psychology, social work, and public health.

The definition of MI has evolved over the years. In the most recent edition, Miller and Rollnick (2012) state:

Motivational interviewing is a collaborative, goal-oriented style of communication with particular attention to the language of change. It is designed to strengthen personal motivation for and commitment to a specific goal by eliciting and exploring the person's own reasons for change within an atmosphere of acceptance and compassion.

NEUROBIOLOGY

What makes *Connecting Paradigms* different from other presentations of MI is the integration of neurobiology to provide a deeper understanding of the neurological processes that facilitate change and growth. Advances in neurobiology have provided an explosion of knowledge about the brain. My goal in including neurobiology is to offer the reader a more holistic conceptualization of those we work with and their struggles.

Understanding the science behind MI and trauma helps to deepen understanding of MI strategies. Our evolving understanding of neurobiology brings to light the scientific challenge of changing human behavior: Changing behavior requires physical changes in the brain. Neurobiology is a critical part of every chapter in this book, providing an opportunity to dig deeper into developments in neuroscience and fully appreciate what MI strategies and trauma-informed approaches could accomplish.

SUPPORTING PARADIGMS

While trauma-informed care, MI, and neurobiology are the organizing paradigms for this book, there are a few others that play critical supporting roles. The science of epigenetics will help show how trauma and the environment affect neurobiology and shed light on influential factors that set the stage for healing and growth. Attachment theory provides us with a framework to examine brain development in childhood, shows how trauma in the home environment affects development, and explains the role and effects of relationship templates.

The stages of change model provides a context for understanding both the process and neurobiology of change and how we can position our services to maximize their effectiveness. Harm reduction provides a philosophic foundation supporting the application of MI skills and approaches, which also align with trauma-informed principles. Finally, mindfulness is presented as a set of skills that heal the neurobiological damage of trauma and establish the focus necessary for realizing difficult changes.

While these concepts play a supporting role, they are all critical to the overall journey of change and healing. *Connecting Paradigms* brings these concepts together like pieces of a puzzle. When viewed alone, each piece is critical to achieving the desired outcome; together they complete a comprehensive approach to helping clients with histories of past trauma.

A FINAL WORD BEFORE WE BEGIN

Connecting Paradigms is filled with hope. At the same time, it is impossible to talk about trauma, addiction, poverty, and pain without acknowledging the devastating effect it has on our clients. As we increase our understanding of trauma, we can help clients find pathways out of their suffering. As we take this journey together, please know that it is important to take care of yourself.

Connecting Paradigms not only discusses our clients; it speaks to our experiences and the lives of those we love. I view the exploration of trauma and suffering as a roller coaster ride. We must go down into the pain to understand it, but always hold on to the goal of coming back up and asking, "How can I use this to help people change their lives?"

If on the way down, it gets too close to home, take a break, a deep breath or two, or a walk around the block, or share the experience with a friend or loved one. For some, this book might bring up issues. If that is the case, please consider talking to a mental-health professional. Seeking this help is no sign of weakness. Instead, it is an opportunity to build strength and wisdom. Trauma touches us all, and the support we receive will profoundly determine whether the traumatic event has power over us or is transformed into resiliency.

Our journey together is an important one and one that has changed my view of myself and the world. I hope these insights will help you in your work and life. Thank you for setting off with me on this exploration of transformative science and healing.

CHAPTER 1
THE TRAUMA-INFORMED PARADIGM

Why?

As a young counselor and therapist, *why* dominated my thinking. *Why* does a mom who knows she will lose her children to social services if she has one more positive drug screen still get high? *Why* does someone struggling with homelessness not get a job? *Why* won't someone living with HIV take medication that will save their lives? *Why* do my clients keep making destructive choices when there is every reason in the world to change their behavior? It broke my heart to watch people destroyed by their choices, and I hated feeling powerless to help them in any meaningful way.

When we lack the ability to understand the *why* behind a behavior, we pass harsh judgment on the person. The restless kid in school becomes the "bad kid." The person struggling with drug abuse becomes a "weak and sick addict." The person living on the streets becomes an "unmotivated, lazy drain on our community."

In the first days of my helping career, a contradiction struck me; I enjoyed and valued my clients as people, and at the same time disapproved of their behaviors. Getting to know them, I found them to be good people with hopes and dreams beyond their current situations. The problem was that their behaviors locked them in destructive cycles that often led to homelessness, prison, poverty, violence, and addiction.

Why were people with a whole lot of good inside of them engaging in such destructive and illogical behaviors?

Answers began to formulate when I started to explore the science of stress and trauma. If the question is "Why do my clients struggle to make healthy choices and change destructive behaviors?", then the answer is straightforward: "Because of their history of trauma and the current level of stress in their lives." Can it be that simple?

DEFINING TRAUMA

Connecting Paradigms will discuss several types of stress and trauma. First, big T trauma, or a traumatic event, is what is commonly just referred to as trauma. Something terrible happens that overcomes the person's ability to cope and maintain emotional regulation. Trauma knocks someone down and keeps them there for a period until they receive help to recover and grow from the experience.

There is also a phenomenon I will call small t trauma. Small t trauma occurs when someone lives in highly stressful situations for extended periods of time (Lewis, 2006; Siebert, 2005). Big T traumas are associated with a specific time and place; small t traumas lack this specificity but have an equally devastating effect.

Think about the stress that many clients face: violent homes or neighborhoods, poverty, housing and food instability, systems that are difficult to navigate, chronic diseases, and struggles in employment and educational settings. Understanding all the stresses that clients face in their lives can enable us to provide empathy and understanding when they react with intense frustration and escalated behavior.

Here is a quick example to show the relationship between big T trauma and small t trauma.

A client experiencing homelessness is assaulted at 3:30 pm on a Tuesday afternoon while trying to sleep in the park. Her assailants steal all her belongings, and she goes to the emergency room due to the severity of her injuries. The assault and theft are a big T trauma, as we can point to a time and place where it happened.

Now let's examine how the client experiences small t trauma in the hours leading up to the traumatic event. The Monday before the trauma, the client woke up in a homeless shelter. The client did not know where or if she would be able to get a meal, whether she would be safe taking a nap in the park, and whether she would get a shelter bed at the end of the day or be forced to sleep outside in the cold.

There was not a traumatic event before Tuesday's assault and theft. However, the dangers and lack of safety and security that create small t trauma have similar biological and psychological consequences as big T trauma. When one experiences homelessness, war, or living in a violent neighborhood or home, there might not always be an event at a specific time and place that we can identify as traumatic, but the constant threat of a possible trauma becomes traumatic in and of itself.

Complex trauma is trauma that occurs systematically over time and involves a combination of big T and small t traumas. Examples of complex trauma would be a child who experiences sexual abuse over several years by a family member, or someone living in a home where domestic violence is a common occurrence. Complex trauma dominates the life of the survivor. The brains of those experiencing complex trauma develop around surviving the abuse, robbing energy from developmental processes that support emotional regulation and cognitive engagement (Bloom & Farragher, 2011; Herman, 1997).

Big T and small t traumas have similar effects on brain functioning, psychological health, medical well-being, and relationships with others (Nakazawa, 2016). Throughout *Connecting Paradigms,* the word trauma will be used to describe both big T and small t traumas unless otherwise noted. Whether a trauma happens as a big event or affects the client over time, the result is a life dominated by the pain and suffering associated with the experience.

THE TRAUMA-INFORMED PARADIGM

The trauma-informed paradigm challenges many long-ingrained beliefs and approaches in psychology, social work, education, and health care. A quote from Buddhist monk Thich Nhat Hanh (2006) describing Buddha captures the spirit and methodology of the trauma-informed paradigm in a beautiful and concise way. While he is talking about Buddha, I am talking about you as a helper. The name Buddha can be replaced with nurse, teacher, case manager, therapist, coach, or another helping label.

> *When I was a novice, I could not understand why, if the world is filled with suffering, the Buddha has such a beautiful smile. Why isn't he disturbed by all the suffering? Later I discovered that the Buddha has enough understanding, calm, and strength; that is why the suffering does not overwhelm him. He is able to smile to suffering because he knows how to take care of it and to help transform it. We need to be aware of the suffering, but retain our clarity, calmness, and strength so we can help transform the situation. The ocean of tears cannot drown us if karuna is there. That is*

why the Buddha's smile is possible.

Note: Karuna translates as compassion.

Let's dig deeper into this quote, as it will guide our exploration of the trauma-informed paradigm.

Later I discovered that the Buddha has enough understanding, calm, and strength; that is why the suffering does not overwhelm him.

The phrase *trauma-informed*, in the context of trauma-informed care, trauma-informed schools, and trauma-informed policies, challenges us to acquire a thorough understanding of the science and research about the effects of trauma. Our understanding of suffering allows us to see trauma not as a permanent state of being, but as a chapter in the overall story of someone's life. While the chapter on trauma is painful, it does not have to dominate the rest of the story and, if transformed, can become a source of wisdom and strength.

Trauma knowledge and understanding is just one aspect of working with trauma. We now know that the pain, suffering, and hopelessness of a client struggling with trauma can transfer to an empathetic and compassionate helper. The terms used to describe these transfers are secondary or vicarious trauma (Lipsky & Burk, 2009). As helpers, we are called to bring a sense of calm into our work with clients. A burnt-out or traumatized helper does more harm than good and can rob the client of a healing opportunity.

Being a helper is a challenging and influential role; as we'll see throughout *Connecting Paradigms*, our strength is critical to both our health and the outcomes of our clients. Healing and change rise out of relationships based on a foundation of trust. As the helper, we must be worthy of the trust of our clients, many of whom have been traumatized by people and systems that were supposed to help, protect, and care for them.

He can smile to suffering because he knows how to take care of it and to help transform it. We need to be aware of the suffering, but retain our clarity, calmness, and strength so we can help transform the situation.

The central theme of *Connecting Paradigms* is that recovering from trauma is an opportunity to acquire strength and wisdom. Every traumatic event causes a significant amount of pain and suffering. With the right mix of support and resources, resiliency can replace this pain.

Most people can identify a tough time in their life. Maybe you would label this as a big T or small t trauma or just a tough chapter in your life story. If you feel like you have overcome this tough time, you probably relate to the statement, "I would never want to go through that hell again, but I am a stronger person today for having survived that experience."

This transformation of pain and suffering to strength and wisdom is post-traumatic growth. The pain of the experience is behind us, and we no longer feel controlled or negatively affected by it. At the same time, we carry the confidence and wisdom of our survival with us as a source of resiliency that we can use to overcome future difficulties and challenges.

As we explore the science of trauma, please keep in mind that those of us who have become stronger for overcoming our past trauma are the lucky ones. So many of those who struggle with addiction, homelessness, unemployment, poverty, and other hardships have not had the right mix of support and resources to transform their pain and suffering into strength and wisdom. In other words, they are still living every day with the unresolved pain of their past.

> *... so we can help transform the situation.*

Traumatic transformation is a beautiful process where a stronger and more resilient person emerges from tremendous pain and suffering. As helpers, we are critical to this process. Transformation, healing, and change happen only in the context of healthy and compassionate relationships. The process of transforming pain and suffering to strength and wisdom is a complicated process that will require a different mix of variables for each person. However, the one variable that must be present for true transformation to occur is that someone must care deeply about the person. To put it simply, YOU are that key variable.

> *The ocean of tears cannot drown us if karuna is there. That is why the Buddha's smile is possible.*

Trauma is ugly, painful, debilitating, and destructive. On the surface, it is the most depressing topic one can tackle. When seen as an opportunity to become stronger and wiser, trauma becomes less of a state of being and more a potential for growth. As helpers, we bring light to darkness, hope to resignation, compassion to shame, and value to worthlessness. We signed up to work in the *ocean of tears*, but our skills and compassion carry the power to transform and heal.

THE ADVERSE CHILDHOOD EXPERIENCE STUDY

The study that started the trauma-informed paradigm was the Adverse Childhood Experience Study or ACE Study. The ACE Study is a collaborative research study between Kaiser Permanente and the Centers for Disease Control and Prevention. Over 17,000 Kaiser patients in San Diego, California, most of whom were employed, had a college education, and had medical insurance through their employer when the study started, participated in the largest trauma study to date. The ACE Study looked at the effects of adverse childhood experiences throughout their lifespans (Centers for Disease Control and Prevention [CDC], 2016).

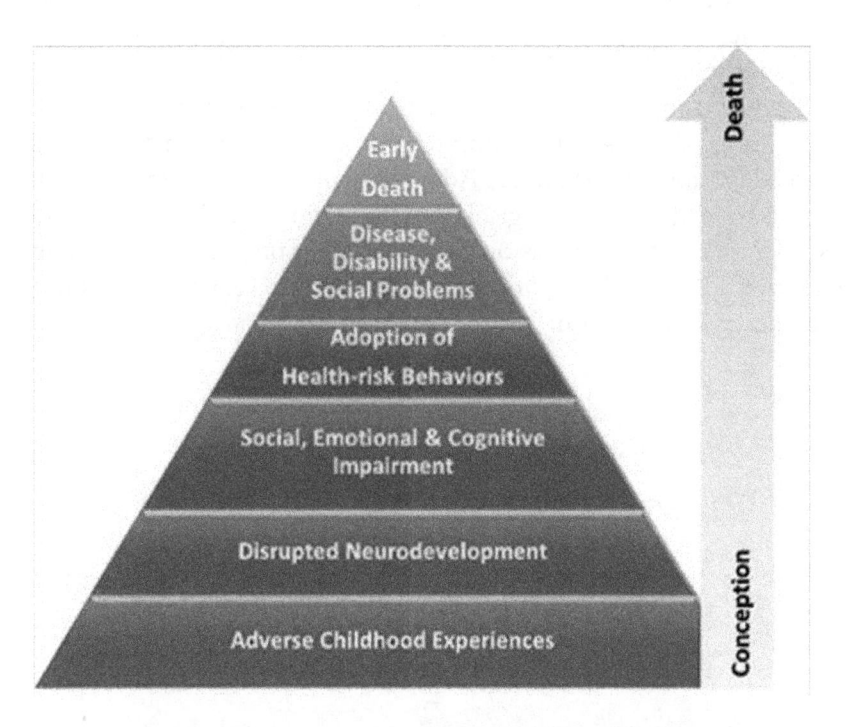

Figure 1-1: Mechanisms by Which Adverse Childhood Experiences Influence Health and Well-being throughout the Lifespan (CDC, 2016).

Adverse childhood experiences fit into three categories: abuse, neglect, and household dysfunction. Abuse includes physical, psychological, or sexual abuse. Neglect can be either physical or emotional neglect. Household dysfunction includes living in a domestic-violence situation, experiencing divorce, or living with a family member who was a substance abuser, mentally ill, suicidal, or serving a prison sentence (Robert Wood Johnson Foundation, 2017). While the ACE Study covers many of the common childhood traumas, it does not assess many big T and small t traumas. Events such as medical emergencies, deaths of parents and siblings, poverty, homelessness, and many other situations that we now know have negative effects on child development have been left off the ACEs list (Nakazawa, 2016).

The ACE Study researched how common adverse childhood experiences were within the study group. One of the surprising findings of the ACE Study is that nearly two-thirds of people in the study had at least one adverse childhood experience (Robert Wood Johnson Foundation, 2017). This finding was a much higher rate of prevalence than previously suspected and showed how common trauma is in our communities.

Besides finding a high incidence of childhood trauma, the ACE Study also demonstrated long-term effects of trauma that were surprising and devastating. Adverse childhood experiences were shown to lead to psychological, biological, and social symptoms such as memory loss, depression, suicide attempts, drug use, cancer, autoimmune problems, domestic violence, sexually transmitted infections, and isolation.

Results of Adverse Childhood Experiences		
Inability to focus	Chronic fatigue	Anger
Learning disrupted	Feelings of detachment	Rage
Short-term memory	Depression	Fibromyalgia
Verbal memory	Suicide attempts	Unintended pregnancies
Narrative memory	Autoimmune disease	Difficulty trusting others
Limited volition	Lupus	Nightmares
Emotional instability	Asthma	Liver disease
Nightmares	Obesity	Isolation
Somatic pain	Disrupted sleep patterns	Social withdrawal
Heart attacks	Constipation or diarrhea	Illicit drug use
Fetal death	Fear	Smoking
Stroke	Anxiety	Attachment issues
Cancer	Diabetes	Flashbacks
Concern about burdening others with problems	Risk for intimate partner violence	Lack of awareness of social cues
Sexually transmitted infections (STIs)	Increased number of emergency room visits	Alcohol abuse & dependence
Decreased health-related quality of life	Disrupted personality development	Loss of positive point of view (self & world)
(*Sources:* CDC, 2016; Herman, 1997; Robert Wood Johnson Foundation, 2017; Levin, 2004; Nakazawa, 2016.)		

The study also showed that the more ACEs one has, the more risk behaviors and associated health outcomes occurred. The ACE Study results show that those who experience six or more ACEs have a life expectancy of 60 years compared to 80 years for those with no ACEs. ACEs are prevalent and they can affect the person throughout their lifespan (Nakazawa, 2016). The next question is "Why do they have this effect?"

Around the same time that the ACE Study started, scientific knowledge about the brain was expanding. As medical technology advanced, scientists could investigate the brain in much more detail and depth than ever before. When ACE researchers asked the question, "Why do adverse childhood experiences lead to behavioral and health issues?", neurobiology research, or the science of the nervous system, started to provide answers. Brain scans of trauma victims documented disrupted neurodevelopment that helped explain the social, emotional, and cognitive impairment often seen in people experiencing trauma. Those who had adverse childhood experiences, and did not have the support to recover, had brains that developed differently than those without traumatic experiences (CDC, 2016; Herman, 1997; Levin, 2004).

The brains of people with unresolved trauma showed an overdevelopment of emotional and reactive parts of their brains, which supported behaviors that helped them survive their traumatic experiences. Unfortunately, these same behaviors are often maladaptive in the larger world, making it difficult to thrive in education, employment, and often healthcare settings.

Too often helpers focus solely on the symptoms and risk behaviors associated with trauma. The focus on symptoms represents the traditional paradigm that we are trying to get away from when we only ask the questions "What is wrong with you?" or "What did you do?" (Bloom & Farragher, 2013). In this old way of thinking, the client can quickly lose their humanity and become the embodiment of their problems. Often the symptoms of trauma can lead to labels, such as addict, homeless, criminal, perpetrator, or abuser. When one looks at all the symptoms of trauma, it is easy to stay focused on the "What did you do?" or "What is wrong with you?" questions, which can feel overwhelming both for the client and helper.

The trauma-informed paradigm is a call to change old ways of thinking and move toward approaches based on the brain and trauma research. We must challenge ourselves to stop focusing exclusively on the symptoms and behaviors related to trauma and instead consider how we can help heal the trauma histories behind those behaviors. To help clients heal from their trauma, we must understand what happened to a person and how the experience and suffering have affected their brain. This switch in thinking is key to the trauma-informed paradigm shift. It allows helpers, organizations, and communities to approach struggling clients with understanding, rather than judgment.

With trauma-informed care, the question shifts from "What did you do?" or "What is wrong with you?" to "What happened to you?".

RAPID POST-TRAUMATIC GROWTH

Before ending this chapter, let's examine an important phenomenon. Why do some people who experience trauma bounce back quickly while others carry the pain with them for years? The first difference is that most individuals who bounce back quickly experience a single traumatic event in an otherwise healthy life. This single event or big T trauma is still devastating, and not everyone in this situation recovers quickly. In general, however, it is harder to recover when a person has a history of repeated or complex trauma (Nakazawa, 2016).

The second difference is the age when the trauma occurred. As we age, our brains are better able to regulate emotions and handle greater levels of stress. Something that might traumatize a five-year-old brain might just be stressful for a person in their twenties. Also, those that experience trauma early in life and don't fully recover are more likely to experience stressful events in the future as traumatic (Ogden, Minton, & Pain, 2006).

The third difference is relational support. One instinctual response to trauma is to reach out for help. If a parent, teacher, family member, friend, or other caring person provides support and compassion, the person has a much better chance of recovery in the short term (Cozolino, 2010; Nakazawa, 2016). It is important to recognize that many who end up in homeless shelters, prisons, or other high-level services never had this person enter their lives. For others, someone might have wanted to help, but after years of trauma and pain, the person might not have been able to trust this person, and the opportunity for healing passes unrealized.

A fourth difference is community support. In the case of natural disasters and well-published traumas such a terrorist attack, there is often an outpouring of community support. Neighbors open their homes and their wallets, governments provide relief, and people rally to rebuild and overcome. Compare this to the experience of someone living on the street, a person released from prison, or a slave of human trafficking. Instead of their communities rallying to support them, they are often left isolated, stigmatized, and forgotten (Cozolino, 2010).

In the next chapter, we will dive deeper into the neurobiological research that will help us understand the effects of trauma and how they make changing behavior difficult.

CHAPTER 2
TRAUMA AND HUMAN DEVELOPMENT

In the last chapter, we introduced the fact that big T traumas (traumatic events) and small t traumas (living in high-stress environments with the threat of big T traumas) both affect neurobiological, or brain, functioning. The brain is one of the most complicated things ever studied. Each discovery creates new questions and the need for further research and study.

The rapidly developing science of neurobiology is one of the fundamental paradigms throughout *Connecting Paradigms*. Our goal is to simplify the complexity of the brain in a way that makes it practical for work with clients. Understanding the neurobiological underpinnings that are at play when somebody endures trauma allows us to match our style, step by step, with the neurological changes necessary to support change and healing.

This exploration will require us to delve into the forefront of scientific discoveries in a diverse range of fields connected to neurobiology. The next two chapters will provide a scientific foundation for a deeper understanding of the concepts behind MI and healing from trauma. Due to the complexity of this material, give yourself permission to read sections over several times as we utilize this information in future chapters.

Gaining a solid understanding of the human brain will take some time and repetition. Once achieved, this understanding provides us with a new language to use with clients and helps us build empathy and compassion in our work. We are lucky to live in a time where we know more about ourselves scientifically than at any stage in the past. Let's begin our exploration with the concepts of homeostasis and epigenetics.

HOMEOSTASIS

Most people are aware of the old nature versus nurture argument. The nature argument is that genetics account for a person's traits while environmental factors have little or no influence on who a person becomes. In the nature argument, biology is destiny. In contrast, the nurture side of the argument is that the environment and the people in it mold a person. This argument does not leave much of a role for genes or other biological processes in determining who a person becomes (Shenk, 2010).

Homeostasis and epigenetics provide a scientific answer to this long-standing nature versus nurture argument. The dictionary definition of homeostasis is the *"ability or tendency to maintain internal stability between interdependent elements"* (Oxford English Dictionary, 2017). In *Connecting Paradigms*, the interdependent elements are the client and the environment in which they live. This *ability to maintain internal stability* speaks to the brain's natural capacity to adapt and change, giving each of us the greatest chance to survive or thrive in our specific environment.

A quick note about my use of the word *environment*. Environment speaks to how the physical surroundings of the client, such as poverty, homelessness, and war, affect psychological health, thinking, and behavior. When I use environment, I'm also speaking about the social aspects of one's life. Relationships are usually the most powerful environmental factor in people's lives and, as will be seen throughout *Connecting Paradigms*, relationships play a critical role both in big T and small t trauma, as well as in the journey to change and healing.

Changes in the environment will challenge the brain to adjust its biological structure to best survive or thrive in the face of these changes. Homeostasis plays a critical role in how trauma affects the brain. Trauma is such a dominant environmental factor that it requires the brain to adapt rapidly. Unfortunately, the brain has only limited capacity; if it overdevelops the areas needed to survive in a traumatic environment, it will do so at the expense of areas central to emotional regulation and intellectual ability.

EPIGENETICS

Homeostasis gives us the greatest chance of survival; it accomplishes this through the process known as epigenetics. Epigenetics is the study of how the environment interacts with a person's biology and can express or suppress certain genes in their deoxyribonucleic acid, or DNA. Most of us learned in school that the DNA we get from our parents determines our eye color, height, and the color of our skin. This type of DNA is chromosomal DNA and only accounts for less than 2% of our total DNA (Wolynn, 2016).

Noncoding DNA, or ncDNA, expression varies depending on environmental factors. When the environment needs a certain structure in the brain to strengthen, the ncDNA releases proteins called ribonucleic acid (RNA). The RNA directs cell behavior, ultimately allowing the person to develop certain characteristics or traits. These traits can lead to changes in personality that support survival in the environment (Lipton, 2006; Wolynn, 2016).

Even genetically identical cloned animals develop significant differences in personality traits, and can also vary significantly in size, hair, and eye color depending on their environments (Shenk, 2010). Go to the gym three times a week and work out your arm muscles; over time, your biceps and triceps will get stronger and your arm muscles will get bigger. Put your emotional and reactive center of the brain in a traumatic situation, and that reactive center of the brain will get stronger to help you survive the traumatic situation.

A client raised in a caring environment expresses ncDNA that helps regulate their nervous system. This results in the ability to handle stress, remain cognitively engaged in a situation, and recover from stressful events more quickly (Cozolino, 2010; Siegel, 2011). In other words, loving and stable parental figures help develop wiring in the brain that allows individuals to interact well in the world of education, employment, and other social situations.

On the other hand, if the person grows up in a dysfunctional, neglectful, and abusive environment, ncDNA releases RNA that promotes the development of the traits needed to survive these adverse situations. While the person remains in such settings, traits such as hyperalertness, being quick-tempered, or the ability to shut down emotionally will help them to survive. An understanding of trauma and epigenetics helps us to recognize why individuals utilize survival traits, allowing us to refocus on root causes and respond with understanding and compassion instead of judgment (Cozolino, 2010; Shenk, 2010).

INTERGENERATIONAL EPIGENETIC EXPRESSION

As knowledge of epigenetics, neurobiology, and trauma increased, people started to notice something odd. Certain children and adults displayed trauma symptoms even though they had experienced no identifiable traumatic event. This phenomenon has become known as intergenerational trauma (Hodge, 2014).

Intergenerational epigenetic expression, and the resulting intergenerational trauma, describes how a developing fetus's ncDNA is prepared to express itself. The hopeful news is that the environmental demands can override this preset expression to a great extent. If a person's family has a history of trauma and suffering, they are born ready to express the genes that will give them the greatest possible chance to survive their family's environment. However, if they are raised in a caring, safe, and secure environment, this preset expression will be minimized in favor of an actual expression to support the traits necessary to thrive in this healthy situation.

Thanks to new animal and human research studies, we can now trace this passing of trauma through epigenetic expression all the way to the egg and sperm (Wolynn, 2016; Yehuda, et al., 2015; Yehuda, et al., 2005; Yehuda, et al., 2000). The egg that created you developed inside your mother when your grandmother was five months pregnant with her. For a few months, three generations share the same biological environment. The epigenetic expression that your grandmother needed to survive or thrive in her environment is passed to your mother and, in a lesser but still significant way, to you (Finch & Loehlin, 1998).

The precursor cells for sperm were developed similarly to the process of the egg described above. However, sperm continues to multiply throughout life. Therefore, the genetic makeup of sperm fluctuates by events that happen throughout the father's life, almost to the point of conception. So, while the egg carries the history of your grandmother's trauma, the sperm reflects the more recent life experiences of your father (Bale, 2015, Rudacille, 2011).

Through most of human history, the challenges of our parents and grandparents were likely to be our challenges as well. For many, this meant surviving violence, slavery, predators, poverty, hunger, and threats of disease. The trauma of parents and grandparents were lessons for future generations, and if those lessons could be passed in the form of epigenetic expression before birth, it increased the likelihood of survival for the child.

Intergenerational trauma and epigenetic expression prepared us for the demanding situations facing our ancestors and built a resiliency that served humans incredibly well for millenniums. It is also important to note that just because a child is born to parents with traumatic histories does not mean that their biology is their destiny. Changes in one's environment, being surrounded by people who love you, economic security, experiencing success in academics or employment, and mental-health treatment can all help the person express their ncDNA in a way to promote lifelong success in these areas.

NEUROGENESIS PRUNING

Epigenetics demonstrates how the brain adapts to an environment. The concepts of neurogenesis and pruning help us understand how the brain develops throughout childhood. Many clients' suffering and pain start in the earliest environment, the womb.

Due to poverty, addiction, or highly stressful conditions, the client's mother might have ingested substances, been unable to afford healthy food and supplements, or experienced intense stress. These stress chemicals and other unhealthy substances in the mother's body get passed on to the fetus. The tragedy of this situation is that the rapidly developing brain of the fetus is terribly vulnerable to adverse conditions.

On average, 250,000 neurons, or brain cells, form every minute throughout the pregnancy; at certain times during pregnancy, production can be as high as 500,000 neurons a minute. This process of creating new neurons is called neurogenesis. Typical neurogenesis results in a baby being born with 100 billion neurons, with 90% of them generated midway through gestation. If the experience in the womb is healthy, the baby is born with a vast range of natural potential (Cozolino, 2010).

In the womb and during the first couple of years of life, genetics is the primary force structuring the physical brain. In a healthy environment, genetics can create a brain with the ability to build expertise in a very diverse range of areas. With the right training and support, this healthy brain can develop into a world-class musician, a skilled athlete, or a professor at an Ivy League university.

In infancy, the number of neurons peaks at around 200 billion. During this time, the neurons are forming connections with other neurons; these links are called synaptic connections, or synapses for short. At their peak, between the 2nd month in utero up until two years old, synapses connect at a rate of 1.8 million per second. These connections manage all aspects of bodily functions, including emotional regulation, cognitive ability, and other functions critical to intellectual and social success (Schwartz & Begley, 2002).

Around age 2, the environment starts to take over through a process called pruning. Driven by epigenetic response to the environment, synapses that are effective in meeting situational demands strengthen, and those that are not effective weaken and are eventually pruned away. Through adolescence, 20 billion synapses a day are pruned away. The brain uses pruning to maximize limited brain capacity to meet the demands of the environment in which it exists. Unfortunately, for those experiencing high levels of stress, poverty, or small t trauma, the connections critical to surviving these situations are highly reinforced at the expense of those essential to emotional regulation and cognitive processes (Schwartz & Begley, 2002; Hebb, 1949).

ATTACHMENT AND TRAUMA

The science of epigenetics, neurogenesis, and pruning are all highly influenced by a specific relationship in the young person's life. This relationship is the attachment relationship between a child and parent or primary caregiver. Attachment research demonstrates the effect of this relationship throughout the lifespan of the child. Attachment is demonstrated to predict:

- How a person attunes and connects to other people in life
- How a person constructs a personal narrative; in other words, how they see the world and their place in it
- A range of adult characteristics and behaviors from substance use and domestic violence to the ability to have healthy and fulfilled relationships (Siegel, 2011)

A great analogy for understanding attachment is to visualize it like the operating system on a computer. Whether it is Windows, iOS, or Android, a computer's operating system is what works in the background and organizes programs like Word, iTunes, and Internet Explorer. If the operating system is working, programs open and run as designed (Bloom & Farragher, 2011).

Like a well-functioning operating system, when healthy attachments develop, emotional, cognitive, physical, and social functions can develop in a way that sets the child up for social and educational success. These functions are the "programs" in this analogy. A healthy attachment allows the person to utilize skills or approaches appropriate for a particular situation and to do so efficiently and effectively. Bloom and Farragher (2011) demonstrate the power of attachment: "We understand attachment as the basic 'operating system' for individuals. Without an attachment relationship in early development, people cannot become fully human."

Healthy attachment, also known as secure attachment, gives the person an operating system to interact successfully with the world and the people in it (Ainsworth, Blehar, Waters, & Wall, 2015). A secure attachment develops when there exists enough safety and connection between caregiver and child to allow for a natural development of the brain's ability to regulate emotional, cognitive, and social functioning. Typical characteristics of a secure attachment are reaching intellectual potential, the development of healthy relationships, the ability to regulate emotions, the development of strong self-esteem, and the ability to appropriately share feelings with others (Bloom & Farragher, 2011; Cozolino, 2010).

A secure attachment allows the child to begin a lifelong process of exploring the world appropriate to their developmental stage. Along with emotional independence, the child learns how to take care of their physical and economic needs. From simple things like feeding one's self to being able to move out of their childhood home, a secure attachment provides the support necessary to evolve through the stages of child development. The result is an independent adult who is well equipped to build the relationships required for success in employment and other social situations.

TRAUMA AND RELATIONSHIP TEMPLATES

If trauma occurs in the attachment relationship, the brain starts operating like a computer with a virus. When a computer has a virus, programs do not perform the way they were originally designed to work. Instead of emotional regulation and cognitive development, the brain must put its energy toward functions that support survival. The development of these reactive regions of the brain helps the child survive abuse or neglect, but when placed in other social situations like school, these reactive behaviors are seen as maladaptive (Siegel, 2011).

Trauma with the attachment figure takes away any sense of having a secure attachment, but not the innate need for one. Without a secure template, the person will seek relationships with peers and other adults to replace the safety and security lost due to trauma with their parental figures. Some find this security through gangs, sexual relationships with much older and unhealthy partners, or joining peer groups organized around drugs or crime.

Unfortunately, many people who were not able to establish a secure attachment as a child spend their entire life looking for a safe and nurturing relationship. Often their attachment relationships leave them thinking that dangerous and abusive relationships are natural. They end up searching for love and acceptance in friendships and romantic relationships that mirror the traumatic situations they experienced with their attachment figure (Bloom & Farragher, 2011; Cozolino, 2010).

The brain is programmed to reach out to parents for emotional and physical resources. It struggles to process that the attachment figure is also a source of danger. When someone the child relies on for survival also becomes a source of fear, the young brain has no ability to manage this contradiction. Under this stress, their personality can fracture, creating one mental state to relate to the parental figure when they are loved and another mental state to survive when the parental figure becomes dangerous or neglectful. This fracturing is called dissociation. Just like with a computer virus, trauma can crash the young brain and send it on an alternate path of development, with possibly terrible consequences for years to come (Cozolino, 2010; Siegel, 2011).

Attachment is so important because it becomes the template for other meaningful relationships. A child raised in a healthy home with loving parents can recreate these dynamics with authority figures like teachers, friends, and eventually romantic partners. On the other hand, if the familial relationship is chaotic and traumatic, the child will probably create relationships with peers and romantic partners characterized by avoidance, anxiety, and/or disorganization (Cozolino, 2010; Siegel, 2011).

Those with avoidant relational templates struggle with the empathy and vulnerability needed for healthy relationships. This template occurs when the attachment figure is not capable of meeting their child's needs. Common characteristics of those with avoidant templates include problems with establishing and maintaining intimacy, being aloof or controlling, having trouble connecting in relationships, and being unable or unwilling to share thoughts and feelings in appropriate ways (Ainsworth et al., 2015).

When receiving services, these clients often seem nervous and might disappear or drop out of care if they are feeling they are getting too close to the helper working with them. Those with avoidant templates will struggle to engage in honest discussion about a change or their past trauma. It will seem like they are trying to get resources or their needs met without having any emotional investment; some even seem ambivalent about their futures. This approach to relationships can be frustrating for the helper, but it is important to remember that these clients have not experienced relationships that add value and meaning to their lives.

The anxious relational template is adapted when the caregiver is unpredictable, angry, or helpless in their role. The child thus fails to develop a safe and secure attachment, leading to elevated levels of anxiety, a reluctance to become close to others, and a constant worry that their friends, families, and romantic partners do not love or care for them (Ainsworth et al., 2015). As clients, those with anxious templates will struggle to regulate their emotions when they feel vulnerable or challenged in a relationship. They often fidget or go off on nervous tangents.

At extremes, their anxiety leads to disruptive behaviors that could put their ability to continue in services at risk. Unfortunately, these behaviors are often an unconscious response, with the purpose of seeing whether the helper will remain in the relationship after the disruptive behavior. Testing the relationship is a survival technique for those with this template.

In certain family situations, big T and small t traumas dominate the dynamics, causing parents to demonstrate frightened, confusing, and erratic behavior in their interactions with their children. Too often the result of trauma in the home is a disorganized relationship template. The development of a disorganized template can make relationships and social situations like school and employment difficult. Unfortunately, those with disorganized templates are overrepresented in the criminal-justice and social-services systems (Ainsworth et al., 2015).

The development of a disorganized attachment style results in a chaotic combination of relational behaviors that often contradict each other. These extreme contradictions leave those around the client, including the helper, confused and frustrated.

The disorganized world is one that alternates between rigidity and chaos; it is an all-or-nothing game. Clients with disorganized attachments will attempt to set rigid rules for themselves that they do not have the internal resources to follow. When they stray outside these rigid rules, they often end up binging and going to the extreme opposite direction that those rules were designed to prohibit (Cozolino, 2010; Siegel, 2007). There are three main sets of behaviors common for people with a disorganized template.

The first disorganized set of behaviors is help-seeking behavior or dependency, mixed with disengagement or social isolation. For example, a client may appear in desperate need of our time and empathy and may work hard to meet expectations. Later, they disappear or appear extremely withdrawn the next time we meet with them.

At its core, this is a re-creation of the client's relationship with their attachment figure. The client feels a need for a secure attachment and will work hard to please. At the same time, they may have a fear of getting too close or trusting another person, since past relationships have been a source of harm and pain. Naturally, this doesn't lead to positive outcomes for the client and can be very frustrating for us in trying to help them succeed (Cozolino, 2010; Siegel, 2007).

The second disorganized behavior set is impulsiveness mixed with inhibition. Clients with a disorganized template know that drugs and other dangerous activities are harmful, but struggle to access the internal resources needed to manage the desire for the short-term pleasure these activities can provide. This impulsiveness is often followed by periods of self-imposed abstinence for a behavior or substance. This inhibition is not usually coupled with an openness to treatment or other support that would support permanent behavioral change. Without support, the client feels pulled toward the harmful behavior or substance. This impulse eventually overwhelms them and leads to a binge or dramatic relapse, which can put the client's overall health or even their life at risk.

The third disorganized behavior is a chaotic mix of submissiveness and aggression. The disorganized template is rooted in the early developmental stage when a client had no power. As a child, they had to be submissive to survive a violent or abusive caregiver. As adults, they may become very skilled at being submissive to get their needs met. This skill contradicts the competing need to reestablish the power and sense of control that they never had while growing up. Because they never developed the skills to advocate assertively and constructively for themselves, they may be verbally inappropriate or act aggressively. This aggressive behavior mirrors the behavior they witnessed from their attachment figure, which was how they learned to get what they needed (Cozolino, 2010; Siegel, 2007).

No relationship template is a life sentence. With treatment and perseverance, a person can restructure their brain and become stronger as a response to the hardships experienced earlier in life. People are only victims of the attachment style when they don't get the necessary treatment required to heal and grow.

HEALING RELATIONSHIPS

Recovery can take place only within the context of relationships; it cannot occur in isolation. In her renewed connections with other people, the survivor re-creates the psychological faculties that were damaged or deformed by the traumatic experience (Herman, 1997).

Big T, small t, and intergenerational trauma pull the young mind in many different directions, making it hard to find any stability and coherence in thought and emotion. This lack of stability and coherence is behind the anxious, avoidant, and disorganized relationships we see in clients with trauma histories.

One of our critical roles as helpers is to show that relationships can be healthy and safe. We work with the client to create a healthy atmosphere and attunement with our clients. Being exposed to our healthy and hopeful energy can help those who struggle to establish and maintain healthy relationships feel a stability and coherence within themselves, often for the first time.

When I first learned about the research on attachment and intergenerational trauma, I realized that as a therapist, one of my most important jobs was to work with the client's transference (the past experiences, especially attachment, that the client projected on me as a helper) in order to help them repair the suffering they experienced in their youth. Creating a safe and secure base with the client in a therapeutic relationship allows them to explore their past trauma in a safe and nonjudgmental setting. This exploration has the goal of bringing organization to their previously disorganized personal story of their life and experiences. This process of integration reconnects the parts of the client's mind that never had a chance to form coherent connections in childhood.

This organization, or integration of previously disorganized experiences, does not have to be done in therapy (while it is strongly recommended for those with complex trauma). Study after study shows that integration and healing are accessible if someone in the person's life attunes with them in an empathetic and compassionate way. This attunement can be from another family member, teacher, coach, mentor, friend, case manager, medical provider, or anyone else who values the person enough to connect with where they are in life. In the research, we see the powerful long-term effects of just a single caring person in a person's life. Those lucky enough to have a person to connect with most often build the biology to live a fulfilled life, while those without a caring person often struggle for years, if not their entire lives (Nakazawa, 2016).

What continues to amaze me about our biology is that many of the same processes that can devastate and traumatize the brain play a crucial role in healing and growth. Relationships can damage or heal, dissociate or integrate, control or set free. As helpers, relationships are the vacuum in which the magic of our work happens. The next chapter will continue our exploration of the brain and how trauma influences brain functioning.

CHAPTER 3
THE BRAIN AND TRAUMA

In the last chapter, we examined the science behind homeostasis and attachment. In this chapter, we will drill down deeper into the brain to further our knowledge and discover how this science applies to behavioral change and healing. After this chapter, you will have a working understanding of the human brain and how trauma affects it.

We will start our journey by learning about neurons, or brain cells, which serve as the building blocks for everything discussed in *Connecting Paradigms*. Then we will move into key brain areas such as the prefrontal cortex and amygdala, which are groups of neurons dedicated to a particular type of task. Changing behaviors requires these larger structures and the neurons they consist of to operate in new ways.

Next, the window of tolerance concept will provide a model for understanding how stress and trauma manifest as behaviors, and why emotional regulation is challenging for those with unresolved traumatic pasts. The chapter will conclude with an examination of how trauma affects certain areas of the brain and the results of this neurobiology on client functioning. As part of this exploration, we will explore the phenomena of retraumatization, including strategies to keep you and the client safe when it occurs.

THE NEURON

To understand human behavior, we must go to the microscopic level and learn about the neuron. Let's begin familiarizing ourselves with the brain cell or neuron.

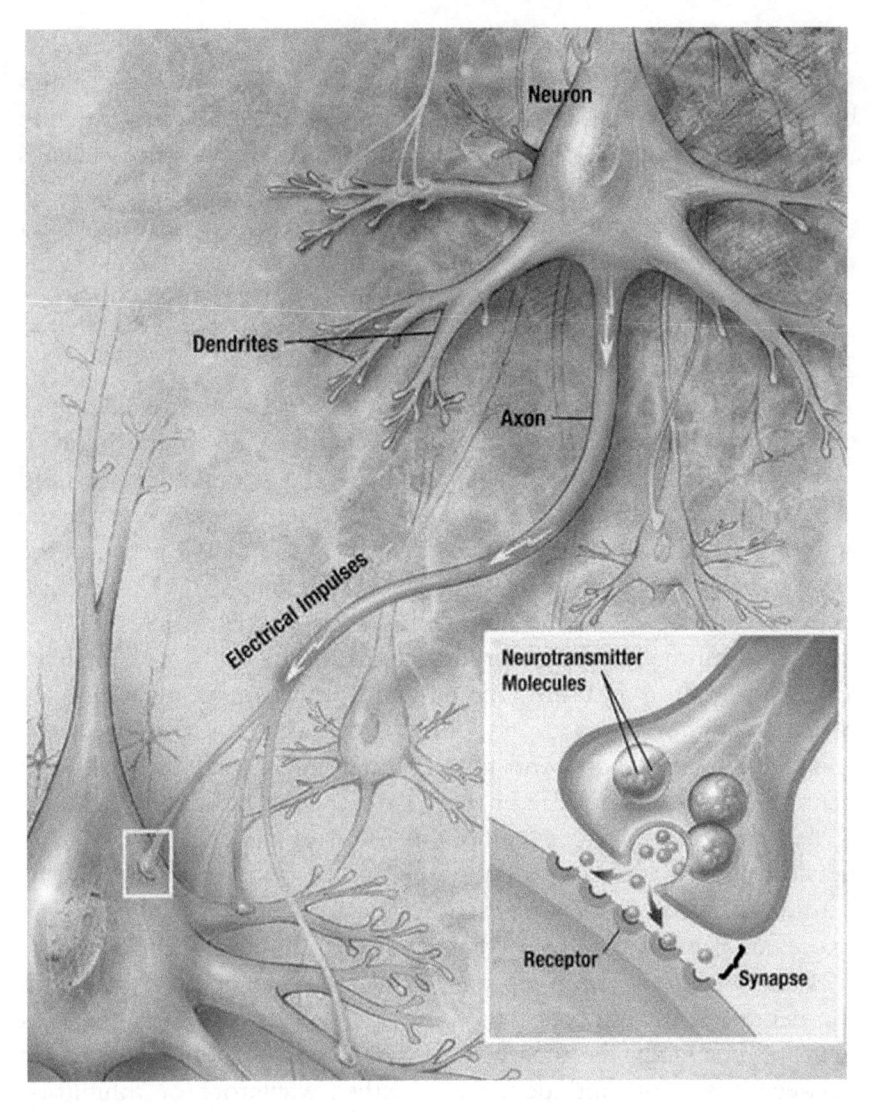

Figure 3-2: The Neuron (United States National Institutes of Health, National Institute on Aging).

Neurons consist of three main parts: the neuron body, dendrites, and an axon.

Neuron body: The typical neuron consists of a cell body, or soma, which measures 10 to 100 micrometers across, and contains the nucleus. The nucleus of the neuron contains its genetic material, in the form of chromosomes, which help establish its function and characteristics (Schwartz & Begley, 2002).

Dendrites: Sprouting off the cell body are numerous multi-branched tentacles called dendrites. The dendrite's primary function is to receive incoming electrochemical messages from other neurons and carry the messages into the cell body.

Axon: Each neuron also has a single axon, which is a long fiber that extends away from the cell body. The axon's job is to communicate information from one brain cell to another. The axon transmits this information in the form of electrical impulses (Pierce, 2006).

Resting neurons have a negative electric charge compared to the environment around them. As a charge comes down the axon, it opens channels that allow positively charged sodium ions in and expel negatively charged potassium ions, this process is termed the action potential. If the charge becomes strong enough, it activates the vesicles in the axon tip that contain neurochemicals. If the electrical impulse makes it to the axon tip, these vesicles release their neurotransmitters, which communicate messages to the next neuron. The first neuron has now fired its information, in the form of neurotransmitters, into the synapse. If the charge is not powerful enough, the charge dies and the information fails to reach the next neuron. Neurons either fire or they don't; there is no middle ground.

Synapse: The synapse is the one-millionth-of-a-centimeter-wide gap between the axon and dendrite of the next neuron. As the neurotransmitters enter the synaptic gap, they connect with receptors in the dendrites of the next neuron (Schwartz & Begley, 2002).

Dendrite receptor: The receptors in the dendrites open up glands in the dendrites' membranes that allow specific ions to enter the next neuron, changing the charge of the next cell. The connection between the axon and dendrite is either excitatory or inhibitory. Excitatory connections open channels which let in positively charged ions. This leads to depolarization in the postsynaptic cell, allowing action potential to continue to the next cell where the above process starts over again. Inhibitory connections open channels which let positively charged ions leave the cell, leading to hyperpolarization (negative charge). If they inhibitory connection is strong enough it limits the charge transferred to the next cell, decreasing the likelihood that that next cell's action potential will continue the firing process.

The more regularly the first neuron's action potential triggers a successful action with the receiving neuron, the more efficient this connection becomes, and the more likely it is that they will exchange charges in the future. This efficiency is the origin of the common neurobiological saying, "Cells that fire together wire together" (Löwel & Singer, 1992). This collective wiring and firing at the microscopic level eventually comes together to form the different areas of the brain covered later in this chapter. This ever-changing brain structure of firing and wiring creates the foundations for habits, memories, thoughts, and emotions. Therefore, changing behaviors requires a restructuring of the brain's neuronal structure and functioning (Mate & Levine, 2010).

NEURONS AND BRAIN EFFICIENCY

The brain accounts for only around 2% of a person's overall body weight. Even though it accounts for a small percentage of overall body mass, the brain consumes a quarter of the fuel a person takes in, both in the form of oxygen and glucose, or blood sugar, obtained from food (Rock, 2009). Being the most complicated thing in the universe, the brain must find ways to increase efficiency in its operation. It does this by forming habits. Repeated behaviors, feelings, or thoughts create stronger, more efficient neuronal connections. These connections form pathways that make it easier to repeat the behavior in the future. Every time an action happens, the connections strengthen, and it takes less overall energy to activate the next time.

Think of a creating a trail through a forest. The first time a person walks in a particular direction in the forest, it is slow and arduous, many obstacles are present, and it is easy to get lost without a trail to follow. Each time another person takes the same path, it becomes more visible and easier to travel. Some paths become trails, and if these trails become used frequently, they might even get paved, making them accessible to faster modes of travel, such as bicycles and cars.

The paved roads are the neural structures created to support habits. Traveling down these pathways can become automatic for the brain. Have you ever finished your commute to work, parked your car, and got out of the car, and then realized that you remember nothing about the drive? Commuting requires us to drive a dangerous vehicle at high speeds, communicate with strangers at four-way stops, and navigate our way through rush hour. Unconscious commuting is a convincing demonstration of the sophistication and power of our automatic and habitual unconscious. Habits are ideal for saving energy, although unfortunately many compromise health and well-being.

Changing a habit requires deactivating the wiring that supports these automated processes and, at the same time, creating neural structures to support new behavioral patterns associated with the change. Which is more efficient: traveling the highway or hiking through a forest with no trail? Changing behavior means changing the actual physical structure of the brain. This rewiring takes time and happens in stages.

BRAIN PROCESSING

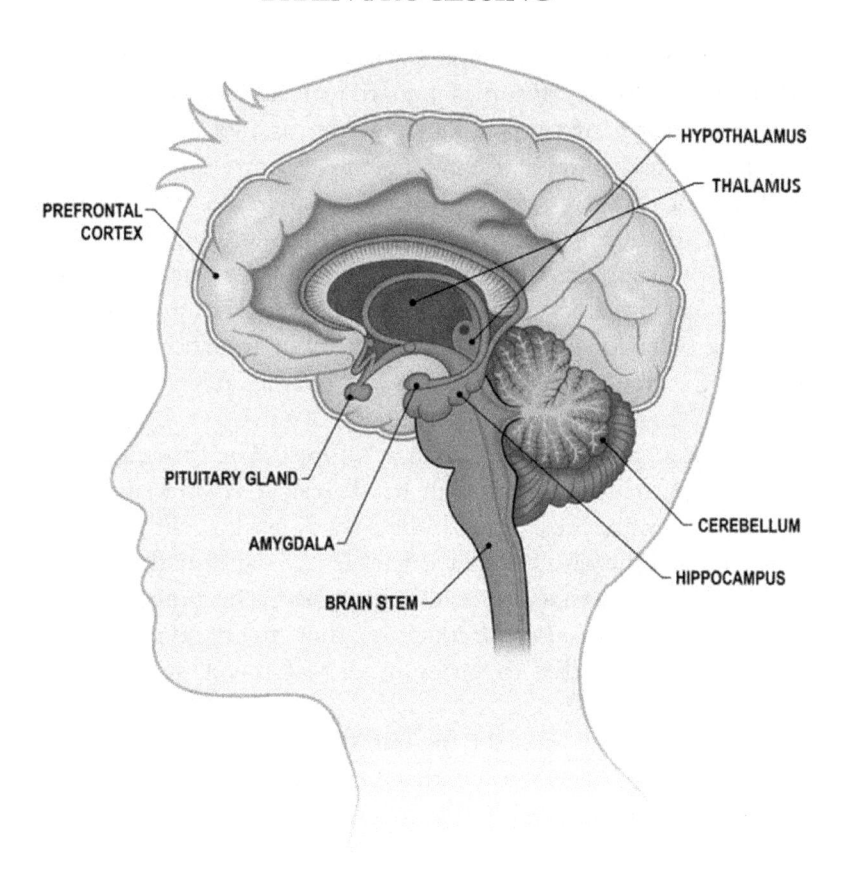

Figure 3-2: Parts of the Brain

Epigenetics, homeostasis, neurogenesis, and pruning utilize neurons to build a brain that has traits to survive or thrive in its environment. As the brain forms, neurons come together to form parts with specific functions. To understand the influence of stress and trauma, it is first important to examine the functioning of brain parts responsible for processing stimulus.

When a person encounters a stimulus in the environment, their senses take this information and turn it into electrical pulses that travel to the thalamus in the brain. The thalamus processes auditory (sound) and visual (sight) stimuli. Tactile (touch) and olfactory (smell) stimuli are sent directly to the amygdala. More information about the functions of the thalamus and amygdala will be covered in greater detail later. For now, it is important to note that tactile and olfactory stimuli are sent directly to the amygdala, allowing for an immediate response if there is real or perceived danger (Courtois & Ford, 2009; Siegel 2016; Wright, 2011).

The thalamus sits in the center of the brain and serves as the control center for visual and auditory stimulus. The thalamus facilitates an interactive process among the cognitive, emotional, and sensorimotor centers of the brain to decide which system will handle the stimulus. If the thalamus determines that the stimulus is not a threat, the stimulus will travel to the cortex. When the stimulus moves from the thalamus through the cortex, this is called the high long road, due to its location and length (Goleman, 2006; Siegel, 2011).

The cortex is the wrinkled outer layer of the brain. It has a considerable number of essential functions and parts. Here we will cover the cortex's role in the stimulus process.

The cortex provides meaning to stimuli by processing them through the lens of past experiences and related memories. If you have learned anything in the past about the brain or stress, your cortex is doing this right now. The information you are reading is being sent through your cortex and connecting to existing knowledge and experiences you have had in the past.

The cortex provides an intellectual context for a stimulus, based on previous experiences. Two people in the same situation will process the event in very different ways. This difference occurs because the people involved have unique memories and experiences. We all have a personal story or narrative in which we develop a view of ourselves and the world. Because each story is different, every person reading these words will experience them in a personal way that is unique to them.

The cortex contains the prefrontal cortex, which is primarily responsible for making humans great thinkers and planners. The prefrontal cortex is central to executive functioning, meaning it plays a significant role in managing the processes of the brain, including reasoning, flexible problem-solving, planning, memory, and aspects of emotional regulation.

As part of the high long road, the amygdala, in collaboration with the hippocampus (see below), provides the emotional context for the stimulus. Our feelings for things and people create a deeper emotional experience of the world around us. High-long road emotions provide us with motivation and push us to act.

A quick note about the high-long road functioning: The above description was used to demonstrate the process in slow motion. In the time it took you to read the previous paragraphs, the high long road has consistently been at work processing each word, as well as anything else going on in your environment. In this brief time, billions of high-long road journeys have occurred.

While the amygdala is at the end of the high long road, it plays a leading role when the thalamus identifies a stimulus as a threat. When the thalamus identifies a dangerous stimulus, it sends the information to the amygdala directly. The amygdala manages the emotional and behavioral responses needed for survival in the face of real or perceived threats.

Centrally positioned and highly connected to other brain areas, the amygdala is quick and decisive when activated. It activates the systems in the body needed for a physical and emotional response. We'll call this the low short road, due to its location and size, in contrast to the high long road (Goleman, 2006; Siegel, 2011).

The amygdala and low-short road activation include the following: The amygdala signals the hypothalamus, pituitary gland, and adrenal glands to release the stress hormone cortisol. If the energy and threat is great, the stress hormone norepinephrine can also be released, increasing the intensity of the stress reaction even further. Cortisol and norepinephrine kick the sympathetic nervous system into action.

Key indications of this include:
- increased heart rate

- increased blood pressure
- shortness and quickening of breath
- sweat and goosebumps on the skin (Ogden, Minton, & Pain, 2006)

Energy shifts from regular functions, such as digestion, sex, and executive functioning, into the muscles associated with the fight-or-flight response, primarily in the arms and legs. In most situations, this amygdala response will continue until the threat has passed, and can lead to unusual levels of strength and stamina. Low-short road reactions lack executive functioning, as systems such as the prefrontal cortex cease to receive energy; this will maximize the energy sent to the muscles and senses (Siegel, 2011).

The hippocampus plays roles in both the high long road and the low short road. As part of the high long road, it works with the amygdala to provide an emotional context to the stimulus. Also, the hippocampus plays a significant role in the creation of new memories.

On the low short road, the hippocampus takes on a calming role. Once a threat no longer exists, the hippocampus helps to quiet the amygdala, allowing the high long road to reactivate and cognitive functioning to return. A well-functioning hippocampus makes it possible to have a brief low-short road response, which might include fear or anger, but it doesn't allow these emotions to become a permanent state of being.

WINDOW OF TOLERANCE

Another way to view the interaction between the high long road and the low short road is the window of tolerance (Ogden, Minton, & Pain, 2006). Per researcher and author Daniel Siegel (2011), people on their high long road are inside their window of tolerance and exhibit behaviors that are flexible, adaptive, coherent, energized, and stable, or FACES for short. FACES is an important acronym to remember. If FACES describes a client's current state, it is likely they are operating from their prefrontal cortex, the thinking and planning part of their brain.

As the stress level increases, processing of information shifts from the high long road to the low short road. If a client seems to be struggling with flexibility, adaptability, coherence, energy, and stability, they are operating from their amygdala. It is important to understand that people outside their window of tolerance are not accessing their best selves and have limited voluntary control of their reactions (Siegel, 2011).

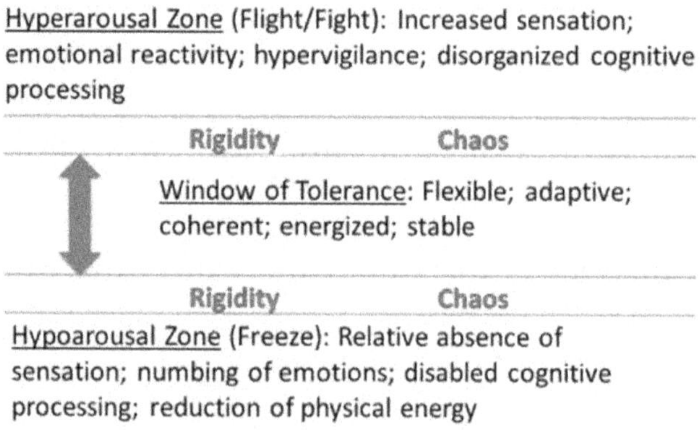

<u>Hyperarousal Zone</u> (Flight/Fight): Increased sensation; emotional reactivity; hypervigilance; disorganized cognitive processing

Rigidity	Chaos
Window of Tolerance: Flexible; adaptive; coherent; energized; stable	
Rigidity	Chaos

<u>Hypoarousal Zone</u> (Freeze): Relative absence of sensation; numbing of emotions; disabled cognitive processing; reduction of physical energy

Figure 3-3: Window of Tolerance (Siegel, 2011; Ogden, Minton, & Pain, 2006)

When someone reaches the edge of their window, their thinking and behaviors become rigid or chaotic. These responses are a final effort to control the stressful situation. Some people react to stress by trying to organize and control their world, which indicates a rigid response. The rigid response often manifests as perfectionism. For clients who have had some success in school, employment, or relationships, perfectionism can manifest as an anxious desire to achieve (Cole et al., 2009).

Unfortunately, for those clients who have not experienced much success, rigidity can manifest much differently. If a client does not believe they can succeed, they search for any limited power they can find over the situation. This response can result in clients not showing up for appointments, being truant from school, or failing to follow through on their commitments.

These clients are not lazy, unappreciative, or unmotivated. They believe that they will always fail, including when trying to make positive change. It is better not to try than to give their best and experience one more failure.

The chaos response is a reaction that allows people to protect themselves. Many behavioral problems result from the chaos response. The purpose of this response is to get distance between the client and the cause of the stress (Siegel, 2011).

A client I had early in my career, whom I will call Tucker, explained chaos to me one day, and I have never forgotten the lesson. Tucker was trying to leave the gang life, which included selling drugs. He had worked hard to get his GED, and he was in the process of applying for college. While this was an exciting process for both of us, it was also incredibly stressful for Tucker.

At one very stressful point in this process, Tucker had gotten so frustrated that he tore up the college application he worked so hard on and started calling me many creative names, names that I can't repeat here. I was starting to worry about my safety as the name-calling turned into threats. Luckily, Tucker ended up storming off with some choice words for me on the way out.

Tucker and I had done a lot of work together, and fortunately, our relationship was strong enough that he felt okay calling me and asking if we could restart the application process. After doing the work, I asked Tucker, "What happened? If someone were trying to help me get into school and get free housing, I wouldn't have threatened them and called them all those names you called me." Tucker laughed a little and apologized. What he said next is still the best definition of the chaos response that I have ever heard.

Tucker said, "You know, Matt, I have a lot of white people telling me what to do." I sat back and asked him to continue. "You have a lot of demands, the college needs all this stuff from me, my guidance counselor is having me take all these tests, and I'm worried about my mom and sisters who I'm leaving in that neighborhood. When I act the fool, you all leave me alone."

This answer struck me as incredibly insightful. When clients, even young ones, are pushed outside their window of tolerance by stress, we expect them to respond with something like, "You know I'm getting a little stressed. If you give me a few minutes, I could take a few deep breaths. Using this coping skill would allow me to regulate my emotions and think about the long-term goals of my treatment plan and consider how my present behaviors might jeopardize my goals. If that does not work, maybe I could jog around the facility a few times to get the cortisol out of my system."

This type of response is nearly impossible for healthy adults and even more of a struggle for those with histories of trauma, due to the influence of that trauma on Broca's area of the brain. Broca's area is responsible for language, and it is damaged or underdeveloped in traumatic or highly stressful situations like Tucker's. This underdevelopment hinders many clients' ability to express the emotions inside of them. If we can't put feelings into words, chaotic behaviors often result (Cole et al., 2009).

FIGHT, FLIGHT, AND FREEZE RESPONSE

If rigidity or chaos does not alleviate the stress, a client will rely on one of three survival modes. The survival strategy will differ for every client. For most, there is a sequential pattern of survival reactions that has developed throughout human evolution.

The initial response is to mobilize energy toward action: the hyperarousal response. The hyperarousal response that gets activated first in most situations is the flight response. The flight response directs energy into escaping the threat and putting as much distance as possible between the client and the stressor. The client in flight mode will reactively try to escape the situation at all costs, as all their resources have failed to keep them in their window of tolerance.

Think about the early history of humans. If we saw a saber-toothed tiger and the tiger did not see us, our best chance for survival was to get as far away from the tiger as possible; this is the flight response (Ogden, Minton, & Pain, 2006).

If it is not feasible to escape the stress, energy is then mobilized to fight against whatever is causing the stress. Fight is a hyperarousal response that can manifest in verbal or physical aggression. If we cannot escape the tiger, we must stand and fight.

Like the flight response, the client has little or no ability to engage with the environment cognitively. In many cases, social or physical situations make flight seem impossible, so the client strikes out verbally or physically at the person or thing causing them the stress. We are often the client's connection to housing, food, and other essential needs. We have power. The power dynamics override the flight response, as the client knows they cannot disengage or run away from us or they risk losing those resources. Unfortunately, this ends up activating the fight response instead (Ogden, Minton, & Pain, 2006).

The third response is the hypoarousal or freeze response. If the flight or fight responses fail, the last option is to shut down. In this response, blood pressure drops, heart rate and breathing slow, and sensations and emotions numb. The freeze response occurs when the client cannot flee or fight back. The tiger has us pinned down and escape is impossible.

Freeze can also be the default response of clients who experience repeated physical or sexual abuse. In these situations, they have little physical, social, or economic opportunity or power to flee or fight back. The only way they survive is by shutting down, and in extreme cases, client can dissociate from the situation to survive physically and psychologically (Ogden, Minton, & Pain, 2006).

The window of tolerance provides a model to help understand stress behaviors as natural, rather than as oppositional or bad. The important thing to remember is that the hyper- and hypoaroused states are reactions to stimuli or to the collection of several stimuli in lives and situations, and are not a reflection of the personality of the client. Unfortunately, when there are threats everywhere, living outside the window of tolerance can become a way of life.

TRAUMA AND THE BRAIN

Clients raised in highly stressful or small t trauma environments live on the edge or outside their window of tolerance. Long periods living under this type of stress cause the thalamus to adjust functioning in two ways. First, a nonthreatening stimulus is often misinterpreted as dangerous and is sent to the amygdala instead of the cortex. A common saying in neurobiology goes, "It is better to run away from a stick thinking it was a snake than to pick up a snake thinking it was a stick." With trauma, though, the person often sees threats where there is little or no chance of harm (Cozolino, 2010).

The second effect of trauma on the thalamus occurs when the client misses environmental clues that most anyone else would immediately recognize as dangerous. Clients with traumatic histories are at a higher risk of being traumatized again, due in part to their reduced ability to sense when a situation might become harmful. Too often, the client misinterprets sticks as snakes and snakes as sticks, leading to a variety of problems with social interactions, often putting them in troublesome situations (Mate & Levine, 2010).

The fact that trauma can lead the thalamus to trigger the stress reaction in inappropriate situations, and may also fail to trigger that reaction when danger is present, explains why clients struggle in social situations such as the workplace, romantic relationships, friendships, and with helpers. They also often experience severe consequences because of these struggles, including unemployment, domestic violence, social isolation, and imprisonment, and may experience failure in systems such as school, healthcare settings, and social-service environments (Cozolino, 2010).

The thalamus also plays a critical role in memory development and processing. Trauma floods the thalamus with stress hormones, preventing it from creating integrated memories of the traumatic event. These fragmented and incoherent memories make it difficult to integrate the traumatic experience into a coherent life story. The client is left feeling disoriented and "different", with little internal capacity to make sense of what happened to them unless they receive a great deal of mental-health support.

The amygdala is also affected by the experience of trauma. Brain scans show that the amygdala in individuals with traumatic histories has increased activation. This activation enhances the likelihood that the fear response will be triggered. Trauma makes it difficult to perceive one's self, relationships, and the world as safe. When this becomes the baseline, more information gets processed down the low short road, taking the prefrontal cortex offline (Siegel, 2011).

The amygdala contains a high density of opioid receptors. Human bodies have naturally produced opioids called endorphins. One of the roles of endorphins is to release a sense of physical and emotional well-being. Trauma often decreases the number of opioid receptors, reducing the positive response created by endorphins. Endorphins are critical to relationships, so damage to the amygdala interferes with a person's ability to attach to their children and others through friendships and romantic relationships (Cozolino, 2010).

In many ways, the hippocampus is the yin to the amygdala's yang. While the amygdala can bring the fear response and energy to any situation at any time, the hippocampus attempts to regulate this response and quiet it once the danger has passed. Trauma also impairs the hippocampus, but in the opposite way that it does the amygdala (Ogden, Minton, & Pain, 2006).

Where the amygdala becomes overactive, the hippocampus weakens and often becomes physically smaller. The balance of the yin and yang shifts from emotional regulation to being dominated by the fear-based emotions of the amygdala. Small microscopic changes in these two central brain parts have real-world consequences for the trauma survivor (Ogden, Minton, & Pain, 2006).

As with the thalamus, the hippocampus also plays a key role in memory development and processing. When damaged or overwhelmed by stress chemicals, the hippocampus struggles to assign the correct meaning to what is being experienced, resulting in fragmented and disorganized memories concerning the traumatic event. This fragmentation is also likely to occur with other stressful events following the traumatic experience, making it difficult for the person to access the correct memories needed to effectively navigate life situations. This often leaves people in dangerous situations and relationships (Mate & Levine, 2010).

The cortex and prefrontal cortex come online when the high long road processes stimuli. But for the traumatized individual, the overactive amygdala and dysfunctional thalamus means the brain overuses the low short road and does not send as much information to the cortex. This neurobiology limits the client's ability to bring logic, emotional regulation, and strategic thinking to their interaction with the environment (Ogden, Minton, & Pain, 2006).

The stress from the traumatic experience and the continued amygdala-dominated processing can physically affect the health of the executive center. Because the prefrontal cortex is under-engaged, it becomes weaker. This neurobiology leads to repetition of negative reactions and behaviors without access to the cortex to bring the kind of insight needed for change (Ogden, Minton, & Pain, 2006; Siegel, 2011).

Retraumatization is another way that traumatic experiences affect the cortex. Retraumatization is re-experiencing the emotions of the traumatic event(s), triggered by a stimulus in the environment. This trigger can be something that reminds a client about their past trauma, including noises, visual stimuli, or something that happens while interacting with a helper or someone else in the organization or in the community. The trigger brings back the intense emotions the person experienced during and after the traumatic event.

Biologically, retraumatization occurs when a stimulus or trigger that is initially seen as neutral by the thalamus is directed to the cortex for evaluation, based on experience and memories. If the memory centers in the cortex connect the stimulus to past traumatic events, the cortex will immediately send energy to the amygdala, the low short road is activated, and retraumatization can occur (Siegel, 2011).

While retraumatization can harm the client's ability to engage and maintain relationships and succeed in services, its purpose is to keep the client safe. Let's say it is a thousand years ago, you and your family are walking down a path looking for food, and a tiger jumps out of the bushes and kills one of your family members. As soon as it becomes apparent that you cannot save your family member, the brain shifts to an intense flight response as your safety becomes the priority. The next time you are traveling down a similar path and you see the bushes move, a retraumatization response kicks in, and you immediately activate a similar flight response, as you did in the previous situation, without waiting around to see if there is actually a tiger in the bush.

Historically, retraumatization can save our lives. In our modern culture, when retraumatization occurs in the context of a relationship, it can be debilitating. How can a client succeed in services, school, or employment if every relationship seems potentially life-threatening?

Later in *Connecting Paradigms*, we'll review strategies of how to prevent retraumatization and help clients stay within their window of tolerance. For now, it is important to understand that these intense emotions are not who the person is, but how their brain is structured to survive in the world.

Next, let's look at the stages of retraumatization to better understand the behaviors associated with this reaction.

STAGES OF RETRAUMATIZATION

The behaviors associated with retraumatization are robust and fear-based. We need to ensure that we understand the extreme actions as coping skills and reactions to environmental factors instead of being intentional. The reaction is usually inappropriate for the current situation, and it is often hard for us to figure out what in the present moment is triggering the reaction. The trigger can be a smell, a song, a picture on the wall, a word you say, or a number of other variables that no one could predict the client would relate to their past trauma.

When retraumatization occurs, there is a process in which traumatic memories manifest themselves as survival responses. This process can happen in a fraction of a second or build over several minutes. Knowing this process informs our understanding of the behaviors we witness and can also help keep the client and others safe when retraumatization occurs.

Initially, clients start out in a regulated state, with the client in the window of tolerance. If there are no threats in the environment, they will stay in their window. When a client is in their regulated state, we have access to their prefrontal cortex.

When something occurs in the environment that triggers traumatic memories, the client enters a readying state. As the energy in the brain shifts from the intellectual prefrontal cortex to the fear-based amygdala, the client leaves their window of tolerance and will start to exhibit rigid or chaotic behaviors and thinking (Saxe, Ellis, & Kaplow, 2007). If the client has coping skills or trusted people they can rely on, those resources can be utilized to move them back into the window of tolerance.

This emotional regulation can be difficult once the amygdala starts to release cortisol and epinephrine. This struggle can result in panicked calls from clients who are struggling to contain their anxiety, disorientation, and confusion, all caused by increasing levels of cortisol. Reaching out to someone they trust is an instinctual response to the loss of control and emotional regulation (Ogden, Minton, & Pain, 2006).

If the stress is greater than the client's coping strategies, the client enters the re-experiencing state. The amygdala takes over and releases all the stress chemicals and traumatic memories, which the brain believes will motivate the person to take appropriate action to avoid being re-victimized. During this time, there is little access to cognitive abilities, and cortisol inhibits cortex functioning as it redirects energy to the emotional and survival parts of the brain and to the arms and legs. It is at this stage where aggressive behaviors associated with flight or fight response or the shutting down or dissociation inherent to the freeze response begin to manifest. No matter the response, the survival energy combined with the intensity of the traumatic memories place the client in a confused state with little control over their next words or actions (Saxe, Ellis, & Kaplow, 2007).

Trying to accomplish a task is not possible at this point. The most important thing when dealing with a triggered client is to get help. Your safety and the client's safety are your primary concerns. Being isolated puts both of you at risk.

The challenge is to isolate the client as much as possible from public areas and other clients while maintaining as much safety as possible. One triggered client can easily trigger other clients. Your goal is to maximize staff support while minimizing contact with other clients.

If you are in a setting where both you and the client are sitting, it is important to stand if the client stands. It is also important to state, "I'm going to stand now," so the client does not think you are taking aggressive action. The key is to be predictable, while not putting or keeping yourself in a position of vulnerability.

While a triggered client is unpredictable and chaotic, you must remain calm, predictable, assertive, and respectful. Think of yourself as a model of the state of mind you want the client to regain. The goal of de-escalation is to get a message to the thalamus and hippocampus that the threat is benign and that they are safe. A calm, predictable, assertive, and respectful approach is the best way to achieve this end.

Using this approach, you want to verbally relay a sense of safety. Often the best approach is to keep saying, "You are safe" or "We are here to help." Simple messages will eventually get through the thalamus to the hippocampus and prefrontal cortex. If you have a safe relationship already established with the client, you can ask them to pay attention to how their body feels. Paying attention to breathing, muscle tension, or facial expressions is one of the best ways to break the amygdala's hold.

Another way to get through to the amygdala is to agree as often as possible. Don't promise things you can't deliver later, but stating things such as, "I know this is frustrating" or "Many clients struggle with this procedure" can help calm the amygdala. Finally, state some strengths of the client. Reminders of past successes can sometimes reach the client when other words fail.

Eventually, emotional regulation returns and the client enters the reconstituting state. In this phase, the hippocampus starts to calm the amygdala, allowing the client to become reoriented to their surroundings. As the traumatic energy subsides, it gives way to the shame and doubt that their behaviors have caused, which can be very like the shame and doubt experienced after the traumatic event itself (Saxe, Ellis, & Kaplow, 2007).

Too often, retraumatization ends with the program punishing or kicking the client out of services. If we can reconnect with the client, it is critical to work from a place of empathy, nonjudgment, support, and curiosity; this curiosity will help you understand what is happening. Changing behavior and insight occur when the client feels supported. Confrontation may shut the conversation down and often leads to resistance.

Once the client feels supported, it is important to revisit program expectations. Even if expectations were discussed previously, it is important to revisit them after a disruptive event. Many clients with trauma histories will struggle with memory issues and can have trouble recalling previous conversations.

Clients often have a history of being given up on by family, schools, employers, and service providers. Retraumatization can be an opportunity for insight. Many clients have never had someone reflect back how their behaviors have affected others. Statements like "When you were threatening us, it made staff and other clients feel unsafe" might help clients see how their actions affect others and their ability to receive valued services.

If we are empathetic and compassionate in the follow-up conversation, it can also help the client connect their behavior with a need for additional services to address the underlying trauma that led to the action in the first place. The follow-up conversation is an ideal time to bring up the possibility of mental-health and substance-abuse services.

Trauma's effect on the brain is dramatic and, without proper support, dominates the life of the client. The neurobiological results of complex trauma damage the high long road in a way that makes considering behavioral changes difficult. In the next chapter, we will examine how Motivational Interviewing can help make the seemingly impossible a reality.

CHAPTER 4
BASICS OF MOTIVATIONAL INTERVIEWING

Even for an optimistic person like myself, the challenges my clients faced at times seemed hopeless. How could a person heal from so much pain while simultaneously trying to make huge life changes like leaving an abusive partner, establishing sobriety after years of addiction, or finding employment with no success in the workplace? The neurobiology provided the understanding of why clients struggled to make a substantial change, while MI gave me the strategies to help clients achieve the success they wanted.

This chapter, *Basics of Motivational Interviewing*, will introduce the foundational concepts of MI. MI provides us with a philosophical framework, an effective communication structure, and a set of strategies that have been proven effective for clients struggling to make meaningful change. For someone who has taken an MI training in the past, this might be somewhat of a review, but hopefully a worthwhile one.

To begin our introduction of MI, let's review the definition Miller and Rollnick (2012) state in the 3rd edition of their book:

Motivational interviewing is a collaborative, goal-oriented style of communication with particular attention to the language of change. It is designed to strengthen personal motivation for and commitment to a specific goal by eliciting and exploring the person's reasons for change within an atmosphere of acceptance and compassion.

FOUR PROCESSES OF MI

To help clients achieve meaningful change, MI utilizes strategies organized around four processes. These processes will guide our exploration of change, helping us focus our attention and energy to maximize our role and time with clients. A chapter of this book is dedicated to each of the four processes: engage, focus, evoke, and plan. This section will provide a brief overview so you can see where *Connecting Paradigms* is heading.

Engaging, the first process, addresses the relationship between you and the client. Clients with traumatic pasts can find helping relationships intimidating and potentially retraumatizing. The approaches and skills in the engagement process help to promote client investment in their change, while building a strong relationship between the you and the client. The stronger the relationship, emotional support, and empathy, the more likely change will occur. MI provides us with a simple yet in-depth approach to engaging clients around their change.

The second process, focusing, helps us create a shared agenda with the client that will guide our work and conversations. We cannot make a client change. Instead, we serve as partners with the client in the change process. In this process, we will explore strategies to help the client focus on their thinking concerning their change.

Evoking, the third process, brings out the expertise clients have about themselves, their situation, and the desired change. Evoking happens when the helper engages the client with the genuine belief that they have the capacity to make healthy changes in their life. The client holds the key to their future. MI provides us with a proven set of strategies to bring this expertise to the surface.

Finally comes the planning process. When the client finds the motivation to move toward change, we help them chart out the right path forward. Using strategic planning skills, we combine our knowledge of resources and solutions with the expertise the client brings to their life, strength, and experiences (Miller & Rollnick, 2012; Murphy, 2008).

Surrounding the process chapters, we will explore the neurobiology and other best practices that will help provide a greater depth of understanding of each of the processes. These chapters will put forth supplemental research and science on how we can implement the processes successfully for those struggling to not only make meaningful change, but also still dealing with the pain from their past traumatic experiences. Combined with the process chapters, this will provide you with a comprehensive model for trauma-informed MI.

SPIRIT OF MOTIVATIONAL INTERVIEWING

The Spirit of MI is one critical bridge between the trauma-informed paradigm and MI. The Spirit of MI provides a foundational philosophy for the implementation of strategies that help people change and heal. The Spirit of MI includes partnership, evocation, acceptance, and compassion.

Spirit of Partnership

Your purpose is to understand the life before you, to see the world through this person's eyes rather than superimposing your vision. (Miller and Rollnick, 2012)

Often, from our perspective, what the client needs to do seems obvious: for example, they need to stop abusing drugs, take their life-saving HIV medication, or leave their abusive partner. The partnership entails putting judgment aside and challenges us to create an understanding of the client in the context of their situation, including their struggles with trauma.

The partnership is something set up with the client to help them reach the collaborative goals of the helping relationship; it is built through our communication style. MI makes a clear distinction between directing, guiding, and following styles of communication. Directing is when we tell the client what to do. Directing often creates resistance in the relationship, preventing clients from seriously considering their change. Resistance slows the progress down, decreases motivation, and damages the relationship.

On the other end of the spectrum is following. In this approach, we just passively listen. While the client might feel heard, the lack of tangible steps or progress forward will cause frustration for both client and helper. Following wastes both your and the client's time.

MI utilizes a third approach, termed guiding. While listening is crucial, MI contains strategies for giving feedback and a structure that allows the helper to provide expertise in a way that promotes an atmosphere for change. Guiding supports true partnership from which change happens.

Helpers and clients both aspire for the helping relationship to be successful. Some approaches suggest that we should not state our wishes for our clients. MI disagrees. There is something powerful when we tell a client we care about their well-being and future, and that we want them to have a better quality of life. Expressions of compassion further the journey toward change and can be healing for clients (Miller & Rollnick, 2012).

Spirit of Evocation

The second Spirit of MI is evocation. Evocation is the ability to bring out the wisdom that lies within the client. The goal here is to help clients regain the strength and confidence often lost in traumatic experiences and struggles in the past. In MI, clients are the experts on themselves. To empower the client to be the expert on their condition, the client needs to be the one voicing the reason and need for change.

Working in the Spirit of Evocation, we strategically help the client to hear their voice. As the expert, the client is the one talking more than half the time. It is hard for the client to hear their voice if the helper is the one doing all the talking. For many people, especially those in historically advice-giving professions, like physicians and parole officers, this can be a challenge (Miller & Rollnick, 2012).

Spirit of Acceptance

There are several aspects to the Spirit of Acceptance explored in this book. The first is helping the client find a sense of worth. Unfortunately, clients with trauma histories often struggle to reestablish a positive view of themselves due to past struggles and trauma. Trauma can leave a client feeling that they deserved the abuse or were responsible for the trauma. Even though there is no logic to this thinking, this feeling immobilizes the client on their journey of change and healing (Miller & Rollnick, 2012).

Change and healing require someone to feel they are worthy of improvement. If the client cannot find a sense of self-value, they will also not find the motivation for change. Many clients come in with a history of trauma, pain, and suffering, leaving them with a negative view of themselves, relationships, and the world. Your task is to find the good in the client and reflect this value back to them. MI is a strengths-based approach, meaning it recognizes that if a change is to occur, it will happen because of the client's strengths and the support of the helper (Miller & Rollnick, 2012).

Self-fulfilling prophecies are the phenomena where people fulfill or meet one another's expectations, whether those expectations are positive or negative. If we do not believe that there is hope for a client to make a change, it is very unlikely that the change will happen. On the other hand, if we believe and share this belief with the client, change becomes much more likely to occur (Miller & Rollnick, 2012).

Empathy is another aspect of acceptance. Miller and Rollnick (2012) define empathy not only as "an ability to understand another's frame of reference," but continue to make a critical point that it is also "the conviction that it is worthwhile to do so." Empathy is essential, because without empathy, we cannot build the necessary trust and safety with the client that is critical for healing and growth.

The final approach in acceptance is autonomy. Autonomy is the acknowledgment that freedom of choice increases the possibility for change. We bring our expertise on resources and help create potential steps to realize the change, but the client is the one who carries out the action to achieve the change. Many clients may not see that they have any power to make choices in their situation. MI provides us with structures where we can bring our expertise to the table and present the client with a set of options that may have been previously unknown to them (Miller & Rollnick, 2012).

Motivation is something someone has inside them at any given moment. It fluctuates with the many variables in the client's life, but regardless, it comes from within them. The more they understand that they have a choice and the capacity to change, the more likely they are to take the first steps toward change. Reinforcing autonomy helps the client regain some of the power lost in the traumatic experience that can lead to a life trapped in harmful habits and addiction (Miller & Rollnick, 2012).

Spirit of Compassion

The fourth Spirit of MI is compassion. Miller and Rollnick (2012) use the concept of compassion in a very specific way. They are not talking about a kind of feeling or experience of sympathy. They do not mean to "suffer with," as compassion is sometimes translated to mean. They say,

To be compassionate is to actively promote the other's welfare, to give priority to the other's needs.

At its core, compassion is the commitment to what is in the best interest of the client. MI teaches that providing support works better than being confrontational. Support is especially critical for clients with trauma histories, who often have trouble trusting people and systems. Compassion means having our hearts in the right place to serve others, not in a manipulative way to try to get compliance, but in an honest way that leads to trust and support. It requires patience and the understanding that difficult change takes time and is vital to establishing relationships that improve outcomes.

WHY MOTIVATIONAL INTERVIEWING WORKS

The best thing about MI is that it works. It is one of the most studied interventions in the history of psychology, social services, and health care, and can be implemented by a wide range of professions, regardless of educational level. MI has been found to be effective across diverse ethnic, cultural, and age groups, as well as in most conditions and situations that require helping a client find motivation for change.

The first predictor, accounting for 40% of the success, is client characteristics. Characteristics include the client's strengths, perceptions, social networks, values, and other variables in their lives and personality. You do not have much control over these characteristics; however, we can intentionally focus on a client's strengths instead of just focusing on their challenges. Every client enters care with a set of strengths and accomplishments, and a level of resiliency. Focusing on positive characteristics promotes confidence to take on future challenges.

The other three determinants are highly influenced by the helper and are at the heart of MI. The relationship between you and the client is the top predictor. As author John Murphy (2008) states,

Research has consistently indicated that a positive client-counselor bond, or 'alliance,' is the strongest and most reliable predictor of successful outcomes.

Research supports that the quality of the relationship determines 30% of the likelihood that the client will achieve the goals of the services they are receiving.

The next key factor is the amount of hope the client has that they can make a change, accounting for 15% of successful outcomes.

Change does not happen without hope that the future will be different or better than the present. Helping clients find hope will be a concept explored in depth throughout this book (Miller & Rollnick, 2012; Murphy, 2008).

The final predictor of client success is the technique or model that you use in your work with the client. Techniques or best practices account for 15% of whether a client achieves the desired result (Murphy, 2008). While 15% is somewhat small, it is still important and may be a critical factor in improving client well-being.

The wonderful thing about MI is that it provides a proven framework for establishing effective relationships, contains strategies to build hope, and gives us a set of techniques that has been shown over time to be highly effective in a wide range of helping situations. MI is useful in the following circumstances:

- Any time a change is being discussed, especially when the change is difficult for the client.
- When the focus is on building rapport, trust, and safety, which are the foundations of any helping relationship.
- When clients are struggling to find the confidence needed to take on the change. Being strength-based, MI builds on clients' existing strengths to gain small victories and increase self-efficacy on the way toward the desired change. Self-efficacy is the confidence the client has in their own ability to achieve the change (Bandura, 1988).
- When clients are struggling to find hope and a vision for a better future.
- When you need to strategically structure conversations concerning change. MI provides a language to talk about and build motivation for positive life changes (Miller & Rollnick, 2012).

AMBIVALENCE: CHANGE VERSES SUSTAIN TALK

Think about a change you are trying to make in your life. Some days you might make remarkable progress; other days you might take several steps back. You might wake up motivated in the morning, totally lose it in the afternoon, and then regain it in the evening. Motivation is not a stable personality trait that we have in the same amount each day or even minute to minute.

At its core, MI helps a client see and resolve ambivalence. Ambivalence is wanting more than one thing at the same time. For example, John wants to lose weight, but might also be dying for the donut in the break room, which leads to the second aspect of ambivalence: the diet and the donut are incompatible with each other. Everyone knows that if they want to lose weight, they need to reach for an apple and not the donut. Donuts do not facilitate weight loss, but boy do donuts taste good!

Miller and Rollnick (2012) envision ambivalence as a committee in the client's head. On one side there is sustain talk. These committee members vote to stay the same or to not change. Sustain talk would be the reasons why John wants the donut. It is his favorite kind of donut. He went to the gym last night, so he deserves it. If the universe did not want him to eat the delicious donut, why did it create such a beautiful masterpiece, sitting right there in the break room?

Change talk is the committee members who vote for a new behavior or change and is the focus of MI (Miller & Rollnick, 2012). In this example, the change talk might tell John that he did well with his diet yesterday, the apple will help get him to his goal sooner, and his pants will fit like they used to last year. Whole sections of this book are dedicated to strategies to elicit change talk, so clients can hear their reasons for the change.

The strongest voice that has a majority will usually win. If John eats donuts every day, not eating the donut might never enter his mind, and sustain talk wins. But if a doctor tells John that he needs to lower his cholesterol, John is headed to the beach this weekend, or he started to feel winded just walking up a few flights of stairs, then the change talk might gain votes and possibly take the day.

Why is MI so concerned with change talk? Behavioral research demonstrates that an increase in change talk from the client predicts actual change taking place. Just talking about the change with someone else often leads to real change (Miller & Rollnick, 2012). Your goal is simple: increase change talk.

In MI, you provide a focus around the change. People rarely change without support and a strategy, especially when the change is difficult and the client is struggling with elevated levels of stress and trauma (Miller & Rollnick, 2012). Trauma or stress focus the brain on survival and can prevent their committee from ever even calling the vote.

RETHINKING RESISTANCE

The final basic concept of MI in this chapter is resistance to the change process. One notable change in the 3rd edition of *Motivational Interviewing* is that Miller and Rollnick (2012) rethought their use of the word *resistance*, which is a feeling of pushback from the client when discussing their change. While they spent a good deal of time in past books talking about how to acknowledge client resistance, their insight in their latest book was that helpers cause the resistance!

Sustain talk is natural. It is just a statement about the current reality. Resistance happens when *the helper* makes the argument for the change. When we confront someone, they naturally become defensive, which slows down the change process and can hurt the relationship. Change talk only works when it comes from the client. People change when they feel supported, not when they are confronted (Miller & Rollnick, 2012).

As will be discussed in the next chapter, meeting the client where they are is critical in MI for promoting healthy change. You might want a client to stop abusing cocaine, to take their HIV medication, or to stop yelling at their children, but if we expect them to do all this only because we see the need, the change will not happen, no matter how many lectures and facts we provide. Those lectures may cause the opposite effect and create resistance rather than change.

CHAPTER 5
THE MIND AND STAGES OF CHANGE

"Losing one's mind" is part of the tragedy of trauma. Engaging a healthy, stable person around making a large life change can be difficult in an ideal situation. Creating and maintaining engagement with clients who have a trauma history is challenging due to their struggles with poverty, violence, disease, addiction, and other intense issues. It takes copious amounts of skill, patience, and compassion for the helper to successfully partner with a client through the difficult change process. Despite the difficulty of this task, this powerful connection is critical, because that is where healing occurs, change is possible, and the mind emerges.

In this chapter, we will focus on the role of the mind and brain throughout the change process. The stages of change help us see how the mind can help the brain restructure itself to support new behaviors and habits. Let's start by creating a precise definition of the mind.

THE MIND

Mind is a term that is thrown around quite a bit by both scientists and non-scientists alike. Some use *mind* interchangeably with *brain*. Others, including myself, make specific distinctions between the two. The science needed to solve this question might be decades away, and it is possible this disagreement might exist for centuries into the future. Regardless of future discoveries, an understanding of the mind adds significant depth to our knowledge of the brain and how change happens.

Connecting Paradigms defines the human mind as a biological, environmental, and relational emergent phenomenon that has the power to regulate the flow of energy and information.

Due to the complexity of the mind, digging a little deeper by breaking down the definition will provide us with a more in-depth understanding of the components that make up the mind (Siegel, 2011).

Biological: Biology is a combination of all the systems in our body, including our neurobiology. Without the biology of the brain, the mind does not exist. The mind transcends the physical structure of our brains and allows us power and free will. This freedom from biology allows us to express different genetic potential and restructure our brain's biology over time.

Environmental: In our study of epigenetics, we saw how the environment interacts with our genetics to express certain genes that determine our biology and brain structure. Aspects of the environment, including social norms and economic factors, affect genetic expression, affording us the best chance to survive or thrive. Every conscious decision the mind makes and every unconscious reaction of the brain occurs within the context of a particular set of environmental variables. The longer we exist in a unique environment, the more adaptive our thinking and emotions become to circumstances of that unique environment.

Relational: Per Daniel Siegel (2007, 2011, & 2016), there is a transfer of energy and information between individuals that affects the minds of both people. Humans are social beings, and much of who we are is determined by the emotions, behaviors, and thinking of those around us. We demonstrated the power of this energy transfer on mind functioning throughout our previous learning on the effect of childhood attachment and trauma (abuse, neglect, domestic violence, or war). For those experiencing trauma, a compassionate and empathetic relationship with you is key to allowing the mind to emerge, thus promoting new ways of thinking and healthier behaviors.

Emergent: If you Google a definition of the word *emergent*, what comes up is

The process of coming into being, or becoming prominent.

This definition perfectly sums up the nature of the human mind. We have yet to find the mind on a brain scan or in an autopsy examination. While the mind is highly dependent on biological, relational, and environmental factors, it appears to be something greater than just the sum of these parts. We know that the mind (our psychology) can change our brain and body (biology) in real and measurable ways. We will explore this science in future chapters.

Power: The mind is the seat of our volition or free will. The power of the mind is the ability to choose our destiny and break the prison of habits, trauma, and addiction. The brain is highly reactive, unconscious, and designed to repeat past behaviors. The brain as a biological organ has little power to make a different choice. In contrast, the mind can step outside habits and ingrained ways of thinking. Assisting the client in discovering this power is a core aspect of MI.

Flow: Our biological and social systems are designed to efficiently move energy and information from a place that has those things to a place that needs that energy and information. The internet is a fitting example of how massive amounts of energy and information flow between people through time and space. The brain is another example, as strong synaptic connections support habits. These connections allow for the efficient flow of energy and information. The power of the mind is the ability to redirect this flow and restructure the brain by creating new pathways that are reinforced through new ways of thinking and acting.

Energy: Our bodies are energy systems. There is a constant flow of chemical electrical currents that allows us to act in the world. Energy is the biological activation of systems that result in a responsive action. This action can be something physical, such as walking, or psychological, such as experiencing a mental state like sadness or having a spiritual experience (Siegel, 2016).

Information: Information is a signal or symbol that provides context (cognitive or emotional) for something we are processing either internally or in the environment. Emotions and memories provide a rich context for our experiences in the world (Siegel, 2016).

The human mind is a combination of biological, environmental, and relational emergent phenomena that have the power to regulate the flow of energy and information. When the mind is active, free will is accessible and the client can make strategic decisions. When the brain is acting on habits or operating outside the window of tolerance, the mind has little or no power to consider future consequences or healthier behavioral options.

Tragically, trauma damages brain areas supporting the mind's power to regulate the flow of energy and information. As we mentioned earlier, trauma disrupts operations of the hippocampus and prefrontal cortex, making emotional regulation difficult. This disruption leaves the client in a biological state where it will be hard to find the free will to break away from past ways of thinking, feeling, and behaving. Without support, clients will continue to engage in rigid and chaotic thinking associated with past trauma.

Stress and trauma shrink the window of tolerance, causing the client to lose access to the very biology needed to recover from the trauma and regain control of their life. The important thing to remember is that the client did not choose this reality; trauma happened to them. To be successful in helping clients change and heal, we must strategically design our programs and interventions in a way that builds healthy relationships.

When the mind is not engaged with what is going on in the environment, the unconscious is controlling behavior and reactions. One critical discovery of neurobiology is that humans spend more time operating from their unconscious than previously thought. To understand the power of our unconscious mind, let's examine what motivates the unconscious and how this can affect a client's ability to make difficult change.

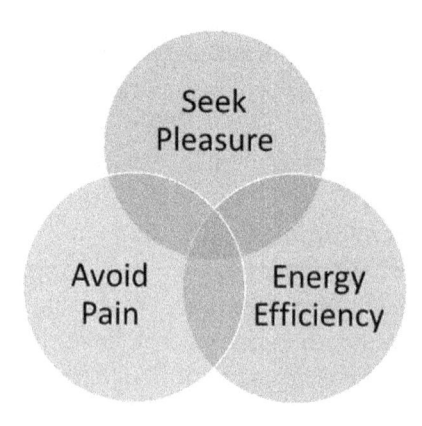

UNCONSCIOUS MOTIVATORS

- Seek Pleasure
- Avoid Pain
- Energy Efficiency

Figure 5-1: Unconscious Motivators (Lisle & Goldhammer, 2003).

As psychology gains a greater understanding of the unconscious, it becomes clear that a significant percentage of our behaviors are directed by the instincts to avoid physical or psychological pain, to seek pleasure, and to do both in the most energy-efficient way possible. At times, especially early in our evolution, these motivators have served humans well. Unfortunately, they also lead to many of the unhealthy and self-destructive behaviors exhibited by clients with damage to their high long road caused by traumatic experiences (Lisle & Goldhammer, 2003).

Energy Efficiency

The brain has a predictive nature based on experience and behavior. This nature often manifests itself in habits. Every time a habit is repeated, it reinforces the brain structures that support the behavior. These structures, or synaptic connections, strengthen every time the behavior is repeated, requiring less and less energy over time (Lisle & Goldhammer, 2003).

This ability to form habits helps us navigate the world efficiently and saves energy for more difficult or novel tasks. Unfortunately, for those with traumatic pasts, this efficiency often leads to negative habits and a reactive way of interacting with the world. Combined with the motivation to avoid pain, this drive for efficiency can lead to destructive habits and behaviors that often leave clients isolated and in continuing cycles of trauma and pain.

Seek Pleasure

We have powerful desire to move toward things that bring us pleasure. A sense of pleasure motivates us to repeat the activity that made us feel good.

Clients with traumatic pasts struggle to find pleasure in relationships or the greater world. As relationships and the world become dangerous, clients can start looking for pleasure from unhealthy sources such as drugs and other behaviors that have potential negative health and social consequences (Siegel, 2011). Unfortunately, when one uses chemicals to self-medicate the pain associated with trauma, addiction often results. Drugs, at least initially, can provide a sense of euphoria, while numbing physical, emotional, and mental anguish. The trauma survivor's world fills with pain, anxiety, and danger. A bottle of whiskey, an injection of heroin, or a prescription painkiller may make this world a tolerable place for a brief period.

Avoid Pain

For most people, the strongest motivator of all is the avoidance of pain. Pain is electrical impulses in our brain telling us to get away from the thing causing these signals to fire. Pain can be either physical or emotional. Both types of pain are processed similarly in the brain and elicit a powerful response to put distance between the cause of the pain and the body (Mate & Levine, 2010).

For someone with an unresolved history of trauma, pain is a constant companion. These clients can experience physical pain from medical issues resulting from trauma that range from chronic pain to cancer or lupus. This pain dominates their view of self, relationships, and the world. Drugs often serve as a temporary escape from both physical and psychological pain.

Trauma steals a sense of worth from the client and replaces it with the psychological pain of shame. How could one person treat another in such horrible ways? This question haunts someone experiencing physical, sexual, emotional, or domestic abuse. To make matters worse, for too many there was not an appropriate response by parents, teachers, police, or others who failed to rally around the client after the trauma happened, leaving them in a constant state of emotional pain. This victimization not only leaves the client with the pain of the trauma, it also makes them feel as though they are at fault or even that they caused the trauma to happen. Where feelings of love and support should have been, there is only shame and loneliness. They may think the following:

- "If I'm unlovable, then why wouldn't my partner hit me?"
- "If I've failed in everything I've given my all to, why would I apply for a part-time job?"
- "If I've only ever gotten the message that I'm not good enough, why would I expect someone to love me?"

Trauma can destroy a positive view of one's self as a healthy and good human being. Instead, the client can feel that they are unworthy of the life they hope to live. Feeling unworthy has consequences well beyond just a painful and pessimistic view of self. For someone to make a positive change in their life, they need to feel as though they are worthy of the rewards that result from the change.

Trauma and a sense of unworthiness can keep clients stuck in destructive behavior patterns long after the trauma is over (Miller & Rollnick, 2012; Siegel, 2011). Feelings of unworthiness and shame directly contradict the sense of self-confidence needed to make difficult change. Lack of self-confidence immobilizes the client and can lead to disengagement.

In addition to feeling shame and unworthiness, the client can also feel unsafe with themselves. In this state, they no longer trust their own ability to make the right choice and to bring the appropriate behavior into certain stressful environments. As discussed earlier, the parts of the brain needed to regulate emotions are often underdeveloped or damaged by traumatic experiences.

A history of pain, retraumatization, and a life lived outside the window of tolerance can destroy the client's confidence in their ability to control inappropriate outbursts. Unfortunately, the less confidence someone has, the greater their anxiety. This additional stress just increases the likelihood of inappropriate behavior, which can often get them in trouble with service providers and even the law (Ogden, Minton, & Pain, 2006; Siegel, 2011). For the client, it feels like there is a ticking time bomb inside of them that can go off at any time without warning.

Finally, there is a loss of autonomy or ability for the mind to influence behaviors, emotions, or thinking. Not only is there a loss of emotional control, but there is also a decreased ability to make new life decisions. As discussed earlier, when someone is living outside or on the edge of the window of tolerance, their life becomes all about surviving the present moment. The survival state is often helpful when one lives in dangerous environments, as it keeps them alert and ready for action. However, due to underactivation of the prefrontal cortex, trauma can take away the mind's ability to delay gratification, effectively problem solve, and see the effect of negative behavior on themselves and others (Miller & Rollnick, 2012; Siegel, 2011).

For most, the world is a balance of good and bad. For those living with big T and small t trauma, unfortunately, the bad and painful aspects of the world have thrown this balance off. Trauma is unfair. In nearly every instance, someone took advantage of their power over the client to inflict harm and suffering. To add insult to injury, no one came to rescue or help the client in their moment of need. This mindset makes it hard to find hope or to expect the future to be any different than the present (Siegel, 2011).

As discussed in the previous chapters, clients with unresolved trauma see many dangers, even if they do not really exist. Imagine driving down the highway thinking that every car is going to slam into you. Too often, this is how the world seems to our clients. The world becomes something to survive. There is little joy or relief from the stress and suffering, and often the life that someone wants seems like an unreachable fairy tale.

It is in this context that a client might reach out for a drink or drug, trying to escape the reality of their lives. The relief the drug creates is both a pleasure and an escape from pain, which motivates the client to use again and again and again. Soon this escape becomes a prison, as addiction, an extreme type of energy efficiency, takes hold and life becomes organized around getting high.

STAGES OF CHANGE

From a neurobiological perspective, the goal of MI is to empower the conscious mind to restructure the physical makeup of the brain. In other words, we want to help the client's psychology (the mind) gain control of their biology (the brain). Gaining control of one's biology is not a simple or effortless process, especially for someone with past trauma or someone currently experiencing small t trauma. The stages of change concept provides a model for understanding the mind's struggle to restructure the biology of the brain.

The stages of change model was developed during the late 1970s and early 1980s by James Prochaska and Carlo DiClemente. This model challenged the way people thought about change and helped to inspire the creation of MI. Prochaska and DiClemente demonstrated that change is not an event; it is a process. If we can identify where the client is in the stages, we can implement strategies to help the client move to the next stage and one step closer to their change goals (Prochaska, DiClemente, & Norcross, 1992).

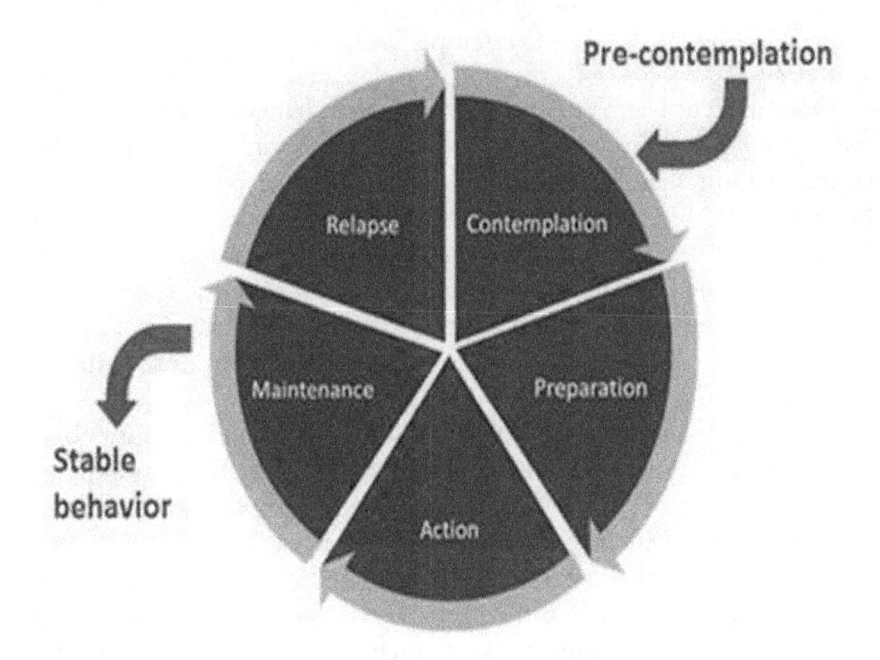

Figure 5-2: Stages of Change Model (Prochaska, DiClemente, & Norcross, 1992).

Pre-contemplation

At the beginning of the change journey, there is no momentum and little insight, self-confidence is lacking, and motivation is nonexistent. It is important to not become frustrated with the realities of pre-contemplation. Recognizing that a client is in this stage gives us permission to be patient and nonjudgmental, and to focus on building the relationship while avoiding being the one pushing for change to happen. Maintaining patience might be hard when you see the negative consequences the client's behavior is having on themselves and others, but pushing them into the planning or action stages will lead to frustration and resistance.

Many clients in this stage have some vague sense that something needs to happen. In pre-contemplation, you want to identify any desire, need, or reason for making a change. Change talk will be fleeting in this stage, but if you do hear it, focus time and attention on discussing it further. This small amount of change talk can often be the spark of insight needed to move to the next stage of contemplation.

Contemplation

Once a client begins to seriously consider change, they move from the pre-contemplation stage into contemplation. In the contemplation stage, the client acknowledges that a problem exists. For clients with traumatic pasts, this insight often carries with it an elevated level of anxiety, shame, and guilt. This emotional reaction can be extreme enough to push the client into denial and back into pre-contemplation. It is important to spend time supporting and helping the client process their emotional response during contemplation.

In contemplation, you help the client clarify and explore their ambivalence. As mentioned earlier, ambivalence is wanting more than one thing, except that their desires are incompatible with one another. Some new clients might just need a little support and information on resources that might help them resolve their ambivalence and move into the preparation stage. Others might need quite a bit of time to fully consider their ambivalence and build the self-confidence needed to make progress to the next stage. Regardless, you should focus on the positive things the client would gain if they achieved the change, targeting the change talk your client provides.

Preparation

The progression to the preparation stage is tricky for both the client and helper. The client giving us permission to move to planning can be exciting because this is what we have been working toward for days, weeks, months, and sometimes years! We need to be careful to keep our excitement in check and remember that the client might be ready for planning, but is probably only to be able to see the first small step, while the larger journey could still be overwhelming.

In preparation, you work with the client to create a plan that helps them name their targets. Any plan needs to be acceptable, accessible, and effective. These measures require that the client thinks their plan is fair and workable, they have the means and ability to put it into place, and that both the client and you have confidence that the plan can work. It is helpful to lay out these criteria for the client before planning starts. Setting these expectations builds client autonomy and empowers the client to be the owner of the plan.

Action

The next stage is the action stage. In this stage, clients implement their plan and begin to modify behaviors that will help them reach their long-term goals. People in the client's life will start noticing the change. Those supportive of the client will celebrate these changes. Others who might still be engaging in the old behaviors, such as drug use, might unconsciously try to pull the client back into old habits. Often, major life changes mean significant changes to one's social group, suggesting the client will potentially experience loss along with the challenges of acting on their change.

The action stage is one of starts and stops for most clients. They may still have some conflicting feelings as they start to give up things they like about the old behavior, and they might experience adverse withdrawal or side effects from the change. For many clients, the change they are trying to make is one of the most difficult things they have ever attempted in their lives. The action stage often entails the client being tested and tempted, and they may struggle with past demons and feelings of self-doubt.

One of your most important roles in the action stage is to continue to build self-confidence by celebrating all positive actions. Even if the client did not make the amount of progress we had hoped for or they relapsed, if they dipped their toe in the action stage, celebrate the accomplishment. Trying to not smoke for a day, going to see a doctor about their medical condition, or reaching out to family members who they have not seen in years can seem like relatively small accomplishments to an outsider, but are huge milestones for clients. Even if they are not entirely successful, the effort itself deserves celebration. This recognition is probably to rebuild confidence for another attempt at action (Miller & Rollnick, 2013).

Maintenance

The next phase is the maintenance stage. After acting for change, clients in this stage work to maintain that change. You may notice that a client in this stage has increased confidence and will start to consider additional life changes. The realization of some of the initial goals often requires revising the plan that was established in the preparation stage, as new opportunities and challenges become evident.

Other clients might start to miss the benefits of the old behavior, such as the feeling of getting high or the people they used to hang around with who also engaged in the behavior. These feelings can tempt the client back to previous habits. Change can be like climbing a very high ladder. When the client is focusing on the climb, all they need to do is put one hand over the next. At some point, they have risen so high that they take a break and look around them. Seeing how high they have climbed can be a scary realization and can quickly overwhelm the self-confidence they have built.

Major life changes often lead to insight on more changes that need to be considered. Now that their drug use is under control, people start putting pressure on them to go back to school or get a job. These changes can bring up a whole new set of insecurities and fears. It is important to realize that when a client makes progress through one change, it does not mean they can immediately jump to the action stage with a new change. In fact, starting from the beginning stages helps set the client up for success with the new change, while preventing relapse on their current change.

Remember, it takes time to turn actions into established behaviors. In the maintenance stage, we should continue to listen carefully for fears of relapse and opportunities to provide affirmation. We should also pay close attention to any unexpected stress and give the client an opportunity to process their experience. Finally, we can help the client evolve their plan over time to address new changes and challenges (Miller & Rollnick, 2013).

Relapse

One stage that can happen at any point in the process of change is relapse. Relapse can be one of the toughest aspects of helping and feels like a collective failure for both the client and the helper. It is important to communicate to the client that relapse into old behavior is a normal part of the change process.

When a client has relapsed, it may be a brief glitch in their plan to change, or it may put them back into an earlier stage of change. They may even reconsider if they want to change, and they may doubt their ability to be successful in change. Often, relapse causes the person to fear that the habit is stronger than their capacity to change it.

Self-confidence may erode, and hopelessness can sink in. When relapse has occurred, clients often consider the reasons for the relapse. They may identify a substantial unexpected urge or recognize that they let their guard down. Many clients relapse for simple reasons, such as being tired, hungry, or frustrated with a person or event, or because of some random event, such as running into someone with whom they used to get high or engage in other behaviors.

Our role in relapse is critical. Instead of viewing relapse as a failure, you can reframe it as an opportunity to learn. You can assist the client in normalizing relapse and understand it as a part of the process of change, then use this experience to help them tweak their plan to address any triggers that might have led to the relapse.

Most importantly, you must show more positive than negative responses to the relapse. Focus on the accomplishments and successes in the action and maintenance stages more than the negative consequence of the relapse. A client's brain structures are reinforced based on what the person talks about with us. If the conversation focuses on the negative behavior and the relapse, those brain structures are reinforced. Discuss accomplishments and successes, as this will strengthen the brain structures associated with the new behaviors.

One important note about the stages of change is that a client can go back and forth from action to relapse to preparation. Change is not a linear process, which can make it seem illogical at times. It's common for clients to jump around the changes or not seem to fit nicely in one particular stage.

Now let's look more closely at our role in helping clients through the stages of change.

NEUROPLASTICITY

Previously, many in psychology believed that personality and the brain were not flexible beyond the first few years of life. Advancements in brain-scanning technology clearly show that this is not true. Neuroscience has shown that the brain is constantly changing. The ability of the brain to change is called neuroplasticity. Neuroplasticity refers to changes in brain structure due to changes in environment, behavior, thinking, feeling, and experience (Schwartz & Begley, 2002).

The brain becomes more efficient through the creation of habits based on past experiences and repeated behaviors. These brain patterns can be positive, indifferent, or negative in nature. The good news is that the discovery of the neuroplasticity of the brain means old habits and unhealthy behaviors can change with time and focus.

Let's look more closely at the neurobiological change process (Siegel, 2011). We can build upon the trail analogy presented earlier in the book to demonstrate how synaptic connections strengthen and weaken over time. In our discussion on the stages of change, our trail forks off in two different directions. The habit the client is trying to change, let's say smoking, forks to the left. The client has smoked at least a pack a day for the last ten years. The repetitive behavior is reinforced by the pleasure resulting from epinephrine and dopamine that are released by the nicotine. Over the years, the trail to the left has become a superhighway, because smoking turned into a regular part of the client's life.

The road to the right leads to quitting smoking. It is barely visible or nonexistent at first. This weak pathway is the brain in the pre-contemplation stage. The client is doing what they did yesterday and the day before, without any conscious consideration that the behavior might be harmful. Each time the client smokes, it reinforces the smoking road, making it more efficient to be traveled again in the future. The mind is not engaged around the smoking at this point, as the brain is designed to support the habit or addiction.

Recall the analogy of the committee members from Chapter 4. On one side, there is sustain talk. The committee votes to stay the same, or not to change. Change talk is the committee's vote for a new behavior or change (Miller & Rollnick, 2012). The strongest voice that has a majority will usually win.

Maybe the client got some news from their doctor about how their smoking habit is affecting their health or noticed they are coughing more. Contemplation is the stage where the first committee vote occurs and the mind engages in a possible change. Usually, the sustain talk wins the day. The ingrained behavior and neural pathways are too strong and the new connections are too weak to change right away. However, even though the behavior doesn't change, the road to the right strengthens every time the client contemplates the change (Miller & Rollnick, 2012).

There is an enormous difference between thinking about making a change and having a plan for change. In the preparation stage, sustain talk still has the majority vote from the committee, but change talk is gaining votes. Self-confidence builds, and the client begins to see that change is possible. Here the mind is starting to take some control over biology as it can envision a future without smoking and the associated health effects.

Next, the action stage is when the committee vote tips toward change talk and there are measures taken to realize the change. It might not mean that the client stops smoking altogether. However, they might cut back to a half a pack a day, or stop smoking on Mondays, or quit smoking around their kids. Each action that supports change sends new traffic down the road to the right, with less traffic traveling the left. The mind is now showing its power to support not only neurobiological change, but also visible and measurable change in behaviors.

In the maintenance stage, the road to the right becomes the main thoroughfare. Smoking has stopped, and the new state of not smoking becomes the norm. Stable behavior occurs as the new behavior becomes hardwired and the old pathways lose strength. The mind can disengage to a certain extent at this point. Smoking is no longer a habit supported by the biology of the brain, as not smoking has become the norm.

Relapse is natural. Even though the old neural pathways weaken, they still exist. The brain can still crave the dopamine and epinephrine that the old habit provided. Sometimes this pull is too great to resist, and the old biology wins the day without the mind ever stepping in. Other times, the mind, drawn by the brain's cravings, might intellectualize its way into relapse. "Just one cigarette won't hurt anything," or similar conscious thoughts can be as much to blame for relapse as the unconscious brain.

RESISTANCE

The stages of change require a neurobiological restructuring to support changes in thinking and behavior. This restructuring takes time and will have many starts, pauses, and steps backward along the journey. This dance of change is unpredictable, and the client can move forward and backward in the stages. This movement is difficult to assess and often leads to frustration on our part.

Much of this frustration comes from the experiences of resistance that can happen in any of the stages of change. Miller and Rollnick

(2012) discussed the discord coming from the client and challenged us to "dance with discord". Discord is a natural client response to the consideration and implementation of the change, and if we can weather the storm, everyone will come out the other end okay.

Instead of being the client's response to considering the change, resistance results from the dynamics of our relationship with the client. If we push the client to think or act beyond the stage of change they are currently in, natural sustain talk turns into defensiveness, which is felt by us as resistance to change. Resistance is not about the client, but the relationship, and occurs when we are the one making the argument for the change, instead of allowing the client to voice their reasons for the change.

The stages of change are fluid. A client might be in action stage one day and then be back in contemplation the next. We cannot assume that the client will always be in the same stage we left them in during the last conversation. Each new conversation requires us to check in and make sure they have not fallen back to a previous stage. If we are ahead of the client, we risk resistance.

Elevated levels of stress can also affect their cognitive ability to consider difficult changes. If they walk in outside their window of tolerance, you are more likely to trigger a resistant response if the emotional and fear-based amygdala is in charge at that moment. Resistance can manifest in one of four distinct ways: reluctance, rebellion, resignation, or rationalization (Miller & Rollnick, 2012).

Reluctance is the first type of resistance. In the pre-contemplation stage, reluctance can manifest as the client seeming unaware of problem behavior or the harm being caused by their actions. In pre-contemplation, this is a reasonable response to being asked to give up or change the behavior that brings them some pleasure or relief from pain. At the beginning of the change process, a client will show some reluctance and even fear when first considering a difficult change.

Once the client moves out of pre-contemplation, reluctance can still affect the change process. One day the client might be fully engaged in contemplation or preparation, and the next might not be thinking about change or want to talk about it at all. They might come across as passive and uninterested in talking about the change.

Thinking about the cost of their change, doing something they don't want to do or giving up something they love doing, is probably pushing them to the edge of their window. Also, many clients with traumatic pasts can feel fearful or uncomfortable with change. We are trying to get them to consider giving up behaviors, like drug use, which help them cope with the symptoms of trauma and their traumatic memories. Other changes might require them to engage in activities like employment, education, or medical services, which often bring on memories of past failures in their lives. As mentioned when we discussed the window of tolerance, many clients have found it psychologically easier to not try at all than to give their best and fail one more time (Miller & Rollnick, 2012).

When you feel this reluctance, slow down. Pushing them to move to the next stage of change might thrust them outside their window of tolerance. Instead, discuss their stress, even if it does not directly relate to the previous change conversations. Often, the client will start talking about their worries and fears about making the change. Spend as much time as possible on their anxiety, as this will pull them back into their window of tolerance and allow more direct conversations about the change.

It is normal for someone considering a life change to need to go back and talk about thinking associated with previous stages. Allowing time for this builds confidence and self-efficacy, puts the prefrontal cortex back in control, and eventually leads back to change talk. It might seem like a step backward, but reluctance is a normal part of the process.

The second type of resistance is when the client seems rebellious. When pushed to the point of rebellion, the client puts a lot of energy into talking about the reasons why the change is unnecessary or even stupid. This behavior relates to the chaotic or fight response in the window of tolerance model. Here the amygdala, and not the logical prefrontal cortex, is in control, and while rebellious behavior might annoy us, it usually speaks to some level of insecurity and anxiety caused by how the conversation has developed.

The strong energy associated with the sustain talk is a sign that you have jumped into territory the client is not comfortable discussing. They might be in a previous stage that day, or maybe something in the conversation triggers a powerful memory of trauma or failure. If you continue to push the client to talk about the change, the client will become frustrated and resistance will emerge.

With rebellion, your first task is to focus on trust and empathy. Moreover, with these clients, you can emphasize their autonomy. Be sure to state that no one can "make" them change and that the choice is up to them. It is nearly impossible to argue with someone giving you a set of options, including doing nothing at all.

Another strategy with rebellion is empathetically clarifying the client's ambivalence. A statement such as, "This week you seem set on continuing to smoke and last week you seemed interested in some methods of quitting; I'm wondering what's changed?" Summaries like this get the prefrontal cortex engaged, give you critical information on how stress is affecting their thinking, and show that you see them struggling. Ambivalent statements will be covered in more detail later.

The third type of resistance is when the client seems resigned. Here clients seem overwhelmed by the change they are facing and all the steps it would entail. Even if they seemed excited and ready for action a few days earlier, when they start to think more about what they would have to give up, their lack of self-confidence might trump their previous motivation.

Again, this might be the rigid perfectionist response, where it is easier not to try than to give it everything and experience failure again. You will often hear "Yes, but…" statements. Instead of seeing this as resistance, see it as a sign that they have just slipped back into a previous stage of change, probably due to a lack of self-confidence or self-efficacy.

With the resignation, it is important to meet them in the stage where they are currently, as pushing them to return to a former advanced stage can lead to frustration. It is important not to show frustration with this backward step. Instead, build confidence by celebrating small changes they have already made in the process. Success builds on success, and with each minor change, the person develops self-efficacy about making bigger changes.

Remember that when the client is outside their window of tolerance, they can easily become overwhelmed by the larger change. It is important to keep the next steps manageable. While stopping smoking might be too big for the client's level of confidence and motivation that day, they might be interested in talking about patches or gum that they could use when they feel they are ready for action. The immediate goal is not to get them back to their previous level of motivation. Instead, empathize with their struggles and work to identify small barriers they might overcome to rebuild confidence.

The last type of resistance is rationalizing. The prefrontal cortex is totally in charge here, but not in a good way. Here the client is overthinking their problem and minimizing the harm as something manageable. As with other forms of resistance, this might totally contradict previous conversations about the change.

Rationalizing is a way to bottle up the emotions of loss, uncertainty, fear, and anxiety associated with the change. We can all talk ourselves into things that are against our best interests. A client might have been solidly in the preparation stage last week and created a plan to quit smoking. As the client started to think about the consequences of quitting and the effects of nicotine withdrawal, they were pushed back to contemplation stage, as the reality of the change became too great.

With the rationalizing, it is important to see the intellectualizing as a natural backward step in the larger process and not as a failure on anyone's part. Use empathy and reflective listening to revisit past change talk. Reinforce that the change is their choice and make sure you are not the one arguing for change. Questions that highlight the client's ambivalence, such as the one previously mentioned, "This week you seem set on keeping smoking and last week you seemed interested in some methods of quitting; I'm wondering what's changed?", are also effective to move the rationalizing from sustain talk to thinking about both the negatives and positives of the change.

Stages of change provide us with a way to assess both the thinking and emotional states of the clients as they regain control of their lives through a series of successful changes. I have had success teaching clients about the stages of change. For many, this provides them insight into their own fear and struggles. I can say, "I know last week we identified that you were moving into the action stage. It seems something has changed this week. Where do you think you are at in your stages of change right now?" This helps many clients engage their mind back into their change and put their struggles, fears, and lack of motivation in perspective.

Stages of change also help put context around the next process of MI, engage, which we will cover in the next chapter.

CHAPTER 6
MI PROCESS ENGAGE

Abraham Maslow's hierarchy of needs has been a way of conceptualizing how needs affect thinking and behavior. Maslow believed that a human's needs are ranked according to importance. Only when a lower level of need was satisfied could a person focus energy and motivation on needs further up the pyramid.

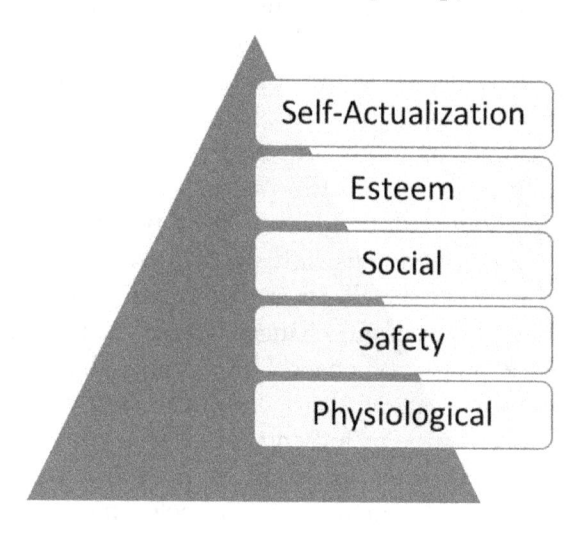

Figure 6-1: Maslow's Hierarchy of Needs (Maslow, 1943).

Maslow stated that first people need to meet their basic physiological needs to sustain life functions, such as having food and water. After that, safety needs become the focus, such as having shelter and protection against physical threats to human survival. When the person met their physical and safety needs, the focus shifted to social needs and the creation of meaningful friendships, professional relationships, and romantic interest. The final two steps focus on esteem, where one builds self-confidence, and self-actualization, as the person focuses on self-improvement and realizing their human potential (Maslow, 1943).

Recently, however, neurobiology research is beginning to challenge Maslow's theory. The key finding is that the same parts of the brain that process basic survival needs also process the need for social connections (Rock, 2009). The neurobiological findings are supported by animal studies on social isolation.

When scientists isolated mice raised in a social group, those mice showed a similar physical decline to mice deprived of food and water. While starving or dehydrated mice died quicker, the mice who were socially isolated eventually died as well, but not before losing most of their hair and other physical capacities. Human studies reinforce these findings to show that social isolation has a negative effect on physical, cognitive, and emotional health (University of Texas Southwestern Medical Center, 2010).

For many clients, their connection to us is their only connection to someone who cares about them and wants the best for their future. The importance of the helper/client relationship can never be overstated. MI provides a set of strategies to help maximize the effect of our relationships with clients to assist them in realizing their need to change and heal from trauma.

This chapter will present the concepts and strategies of engagement. Engagement applies to engagement in services, education, or treatment, as well as the client's ability to engage in conversations concerning their change and healing from past trauma. Engagement helps us to build a strong relationship with a client. The strength of the relationship increases the level of commitment to succeed in services and achieve the outcomes associated with those services.

Let's start by examining factors that build engagement, as well as factors that can lead to disengagement.

ENGAGEMENT

There are several things that we can do to promote client engagement. These strategies include concentrating on hope and positivity, desire and goals, importance, and expectations. Focusing on these strategies increases motivation and the self-efficacy needed to move through the stages of change (Miller & Rollnick, 2012).

Hope and Positivity

Hope will get much more attention throughout this book and will be discussed in detail in the next chapter. Its role in engagement is critical. Hope for a better future and the ability of your services to help a client realize that future is a source of motivation for the client. If the client does not believe you will help them make tomorrow better than today, they are unlikely to invest much energy or effort into the relationships or services you offer.

The healing power of positive emotions, hope being one such emotion, is so important that a whole branch of science, positive psychology, was developed to study their effects (Miller & Rollnick, 2012). Humans are at their best when engaged in healthy relationships. Feeling positive about oneself or one's accomplishments builds engagement. Engagement increases the client's positive view of you as a partner, which then increases a positive atmosphere even more.

Positive emotions and relationships are important for everyone. This is especially true for clients with traumatic pasts. As we have mentioned, trauma steals a positive sense of self, relationships, and the world. A positive and strength-based helping relationship challenges these notions and helps the client see themself, relationships, and their world in a whole new light.

Desire and Goals

Some clients come in with a desire to change, while others might wish to stay the same but are experiencing external pressures to change. Identifying and increasing desire and helping the client establish goals are critical to the planning process of MI. The more a client desires change and views us as a partner in the change, the greater their engagement. Establishing a set of goals and a path forward increases engagement even further (Miller & Rollnick, 2012). Planning is a process of MI and has its own dedicated chapter later in the book.

Importance

Usually, the more important something is, the more engaged someone will be with an issue or change. Importance is related to the level of a client's desire, reason, and need to make the change. Most clients are dealing with many issues. Addressing changes that the client sees as more significant will build both confidence and motivation (Miller & Rollnick, 2012).

Expectations

The brain thrives when reality matches established expectations. It also struggles when reality fails to meet expectations. Shared expectations about your role, the boundaries around this role, the responsibilities of the client, and the overall nature of the relationship structures the helping relationship for success. The more a client understands the expectations, the less likely it is that they will feel threatened and become disengaged (Miller & Rollnick, 2012).

Engagement Traps

Next, we'll examine the four main engagement traps: assessment, premature focus, labeling, and chatting. If not avoided, all may lead to client disengagement, resulting in a decrease in motivation and possibly clients dropping out of services altogether.

Assessment Trap

Assessments, which may include intakes, bio-psychosocial evaluations, mental-status examinations, standardized tests, and medical histories, can derail the engagement if conducted too early in the relationship (Miller & Rollnick, 2012). Let's examine how these types of assessments act as traps for client engagement.

First, the questions asked are often awkward and embarrassing for the client to answer. Many questions touch on past trauma, pain, and suffering that might not have a clear connection to the reason the client seeks services. These types of question can directly trigger a retraumatization response. If this is the client's first experience with you or your program, it may lead to their deciding not to return.

Next, we too often ask tough questions before establishing trust, safety, and the engagement. Often, assessments are done in the first moments of the relationship, setting a negative or defensive tone from the start. Considering what we have learned about trauma and relationship templates, this approach goes against our evolving knowledge. If the information in the assessment is crucial, the question becomes whether it is imperative to gather it up front or if the assessment can wait until a strong relationship is established?

Finally, assessments put the client in a passive role, rather than in a partnership or empowering role. Assessments create a dynamic where the client must answer tough questions to an authority figure to get services they need. This situation does not promote a strong working partnership and is not trauma-informed.

It is often not in your power to change the assessment requirements set by the systems in which you work. Here are a few strategies that can at least help if you are allowed some flexibility.

- Spend the first session focused purely on building rapport. Use information discussed to identify answers to questions on the assessment. Allow for questions that still need answers to be asked in future sessions. It is best for assessment completion to be spread out over the first several sessions and not all at the first meeting. This approach provides space and time to build a relationship first.
- Start with what the client wants out of the relationship and how you can assist them with reaching their goals. This focus helps balance the power before asking the more difficult questions.
- Set expectations that the assessment process is just a time-limited and small part of the relationship, and will not be the norm moving forward.
- Most assessments ask closed-ended questions requiring one-word answers, often yes or no. These can limit empathy and elicit resistance and discord. If possible, reframe the questions in a more conversational tone. This approach gives you the opportunity to support the client and provides a deeper understanding of the issues (Miller & Rollnick, 2012).

Premature Focus Trap

Premature focus entails jumping to solutions before the establishment of the partnership. Human beings love to fix things, especially when those things are causing pain for others. We can often feel like we have the answers for the client's problems. Moving to focusing on problem solving before the client is ready will cause discord and possibly resistance, which is a clue for you to slow down and meet the client where they are in the stages of change.

Most client change requires the client, not you, to take the actions needed to realize the change. It's important to prioritize the client's goals and desires before our agenda. When we jump to solutions, we rob the client of the opportunity to go through their process.

Focusing on a solution before engagement leads to our not having enough information to fulfill our role in the partnership. It can also create resistance. The client may defend their position, which is a natural response when prematurely challenged. Ultimately, focusing too early leads to a frustrated client who feels they are being directed and not heard (Miller & Rollnick, 2012).

Labeling Trap

The labeling trap is a form of both the assessment and premature focus traps. Part of the evaluation process in mental-health and medical services is establishing a diagnosis. A diagnosis is a powerful kind of label and is often required to show that the client is eligible for the program or services. Diagnosing is usually done early in the relationship, creating another opportunity for a premature focus before the establishment of engagement.

Society and the helping professions have created volumes of labels. While these can help guide treatment, they are often detrimental to the client. Having someone accept a label has few or no positive benefits for behavioral change. In fact, being labeled homeless, borderline, HIV-positive, or an addict can have a powerful negative affect on the person and their motivation (Miller & Rollnick, 2012).

Clients are not their diagnosis or label. Labels can dramatically increase defensiveness and bring forth resistance. A person experiencing homelessness is much more than their housing situation, someone with bipolar disorder is not just their mood swings, and a formerly incarcerated client is not their criminal history. We need to make sure that we handle labeling carefully and avoid it whenever possible (Miller & Rollnick, 2012).

Chatting Trap

Finally, we should avoid the chatting trap. Chatting creates a situation where there is no focus or direction to guide the conversation. Chatting is an easy trap to fall into because many clients don't have a lot of people in their lives that just listen.

Ultimately, most clients want to get to the issue and feel that they have accomplished something. Since we hold the role of expert, the client may assume that our chatting is part of the process and will help them achieve their goals. However, if the interaction is not structured, most clients will eventually get frustrated at the lack of improvement in their situation. This frustration can lead to decreased motivation and disengagement (Miller & Rollnick, 2012).

The four processes of MI are in a set sequence for a reason. Engagement must occur as the foundation for focusing, evoking, and planning. Without engagement, the change process becomes bogged down and can go in directions that take the client further away from their desired future. By avoiding assessment, premature focus, labeling, and chatting traps, we are more likely to engage clients successfully.

Now, let's look at one of the MI skills utilized to build engagement with clients called OARS.

OARS

OARS stands for open-ended questions/statements, affirmations, reflections, and summaries. OARS is a set of four communication skills that are central in every one of the four processes of MI. The goal of OARS is for us to develop empathy and understanding for the client's situation through our communication (Miller & Rollnick, 2012).

OARS should always be implemented with the Spirit of MI in mind. OARS is a skill set that helps us build a goal-oriented partnership with the client where we are working with them to accomplish their goals. These skills help ensure that we are communicating acceptance and compassion in our communication. Finally, OARS provides the foundation for skills introduced in future chapters, which help us evoke the expertise that lies within the client.

In MI, we can think of ourselves as miners digging for gold. The gold represents change talk, the precious material that leads to real change. Like gold, change talk can be hard to find. The OARS skills serve as our pickaxe and shovels in this search.

As a reminder, if you feel resistance coming back from the client, it is a sign that you are ahead of where they are in their stages of change at that time. OARS, especially affirmations and reflections, helps us stay on the same page with the client and should be the skills we utilize most frequently. Questions, statements, and summaries bring focus and push the conversation forward; these are necessary but are more likely to elicit resistance. Again, resistance is not a terrible thing or a failure on your part; it just is a way for the client to communicate that they are not quite ready to explore a certain topic or move to the next stage of change.

A quick note: I do not present the OARS concepts in the order of the acronym. Instead, I present them in order of suggested frequency of use. First, we'll examine the most frequently used skill and the R in OARS: reflections.

Reflections

Reflections are an educated guess about what the client is communicating. These educated guesses are statements of understanding to ensure we are on the same page with the client. The wonderful thing about reflections is that it's okay if we are wrong. If we reflect back what we are hearing and the client means something else, it gives the client a chance to get us back on the same page. It's better to be wrong and be redirected by the client than to continue a conversation based on a misunderstanding.

The key to reflections is to slightly understate what you think the client is saying. Think of yourself as a gentle backseat driver who knows the possible routes to the destination and understands that the client is at the wheel and will decide which roads to take as the journey unfolds. We are aware that the client will need to take a right turn in the next mile, but it is still up to the client as to which turn to take. Reflections help guide without directing or following (Miller & Rollnick, 2012).

Reflections are great tools for mining change-talk gold. Reflections come in two types. You can identify these types as the tip and body of an iceberg. The tip of the iceberg would represent the simple reflections. Simple reflections restate the client's words almost verbatim. The other type of reflection is complex reflections. These account for the body of the iceberg hidden from sight. Complex reflections go deeper, striving to reflect the meaning and not just words being spoken by the client (Miller & Rollnick, 2012).

An example is when the client states: "I've tried diets in the past, but it's so hard when Nancy keeps bringing donuts to work."

Here is where we become the miner for change talk. First, you need to decide where to look for the change talk. The client has provided several options to explore. If you want to explore what the client has done in the past to lose weight, you could use a simple reflection: "You've tried diets in the past."

This reflection guides the conversation to previous attempts, giving you key insights into what might or might not work in the future. On the other hand, you could explore aspects of the work environment that make it hard for the client to lose weight. If this is the case, you could use a different simple reflection: "It's hard when Nancy keeps bringing donuts to work."

This reflection guides the conversation to the specifics of that situation, giving you information that might be used to brainstorm solutions with the client about how to stay healthy at work.

With complex reflections, we move from using the client's words to digging deeper to get not just information, but meaning. Let's work with the same statement, "I've tried diets in the past, but it's so hard when Nancy keeps bringing donuts to work." If you want to explore the client's feelings about the change and how important the change is, then you could state: "Losing weight is important to you, and it seems there are frustrating obstacles that have prevented you from reaching your goal."

This complex reflection brings into the conversation the concept of importance and the emotion of frustration, two things that the client didn't explicitly state.

If the client responds: "Losing weight isn't that important to me. It's smoking that's creating the real problem."

You now know that there is limited motivation currently concerning weight loss and you can dig for change talk concerning smoking. You can always come back to weight loss later. Being wrong can give as much information as being right. On the other hand, perhaps the client replies: "It's frustrating to try something over and over and fail every time."

Now you have hit gold! This is change talk and, depending on the client and the relationship, you could further the discussion by exploring the emotional effect of failing by saying: "The feeling of failure can be frustrating."

If you want to explore what the client has tried in the past and why it failed, you could say: "You've tried several things in the past that have not worked."

This reflection will give permission for the client to provide more information. Notice here that we replace "fail" with "not worked." This shift is a slight change, but is a much less negative context. Positive or less-negative reframes can prevent the client from feeling worse than they already do.

Next, let's look at the second most frequently used skill, the *A* in OARS: affirmations.

Affirmations

The next strategy of OARS is affirmations. Miller and Rollnick's (2012) definition of affirmation is

To recognize and acknowledge that which is good, including the individual's inherent worth as a fellow human being. To affirm is also to support and encourage.

Affirmations give us a tool to dig for change talk by showing understanding and searching for deeper meaning.

With affirmations, you are bringing forth good and positive things in the client's life and reflecting that what they are going through is difficult or challenging. Examples of affirmations include acknowledging a client's strength, something they have accomplished in the past, or their ability to survive under difficult circumstances. Affirmations bring forth hope and self-efficacy, and help create a positive working relationship with the client.

Affirmations promote empathy by ensuring that you accurately understand the client's frame of reference, and simultaneously show the client that they have value and that you recognize it. Many clients do not have people in their lives who give them positive feedback or point out the good they see in them. We play a critical role in helping the client see the value in themself, while instilling hope for a better future.

Affirmations are also important because everyone thrives in

positive, healthy relationships. If we are pointing out the good in the client or their situation, it brings positive energy into the relationship and conversation. This positive energy is a key factor in retaining clients in treatment and services (Achor, 2010).

Many clients struggle to separate themselves from their problems. As discussed during the section on labeling traps, we often put labels like "homeless" and "addict" on clients, making it difficult for them not to internalize these labels. Affirmations help separate the problem from the person by showing that the client has value and strength, and is more than just their problems (Miller & Rollnick, 2012).

Finally, affirmations reduce defensiveness. As the client processes their issues, there is a high chance this will trigger an emotional reaction and push them outside their window of tolerance. Affirmations set a positive baseline in the conversation, making it less likely for the client to feel threatened by the discussion.

Next, let us look at some examples of affirmations. The client states: "It is hard looking for a job, managing my diabetes, and meeting all the requirements in the housing program that I'm in. I'm trying hard, but I'm not sure I can keep all this up much longer."

The language presented by the client is negative. Phrases like "It is hard" and "I'm not sure I can keep this up" indicate a lack of confidence in their power to make the change. However, this is an excellent opportunity to shift from this negative mindset to a more positive direction using an affirmation. You could reply: "Wow, you have been managing a lot lately. You're looking for a job for the first time in years, your diabetes lab results are improving, and you've been doing well in the housing program."

This statement shifts the focus from being overwhelmed to the accomplishments achieved by the client. You would want to return to why this is so hard for the client, but setting this up with a discussion about accomplishments helps the client stay in their window of tolerance. Another affirmation could be: "Change is hard, and you have taken on several massive changes in the last couple months. Tell me how you have been able to keep up with it all."

This affirmation reflects back the struggles in the client's statement, but shifts the focus on to how the client has made it to this point. This affirmation may strike the gold of change talk. The client will usually spend the next several minutes explaining how they have been making the change work. You can then utilize these strengths to help the client brainstorm around their current frustration.

Next, let's look at the O in OARS, with open-ended questions and statements.

Open-ended Questions and Statements

Most of us are great at asking questions. The structure of OARS helps to ensure that you utilize questions in a way that promotes empathy and avoids the assessment and premature focus traps. The first key to asking effective questions is to focus on open and not closed questions. Closed questions are those that can be answered by one or two words. For example, "Do you currently have a job?"

The open-ended equivalent is: "Tell me about your employment history over the last several years." If you only ask the closed-ended question, you miss a potential windfall of information that is critical to helping the client move forward.

While questions seem like they are the best way to get information quickly, unfortunately, they can also lead to the traps presented earlier. The rule in MI is to try to ask only one question or statement for every two affirmations, reflections, or summaries. This ratio balances information gathering with empathy building and establishes deeper meaning around the change. The question or statement is the act of focusing on a particular area. Affirmations, reflections, and summaries help find the change talk connected to that area of focus (Miller & Rollnick, 2012).

Statements do the same thing as questions, while decreasing the potential of defensiveness. Shifting from questions to statements is simple in theory, but can be difficult during the flow of the conversation. Instead of asking, "How did your doctor's appointment go last week?", you could state, "I've been interested in how your doctor's appointment went last week." Using statements helps prevents defensiveness and promotes collaboration and partnership.

Finally, it's important not to use a question or statement to direct the client: "So, did you go to the DMV to get your ID, take the ID to the Social Security office to sign up for SSDI, and then put in the application for the housing program?"

This question limits the client to only the direction you want them to go, and if they didn't complete any of these tasks, it could make them feel like a failure. A better way to handle this would be: "We talked about a lot of tasks last week needed to get you on SSDI and into a housing program, I'm curious about how it went." Being "curious" demonstrates partnering, whereas "Did you go?" is directing.

Let's look at another example. If the client states: "Dr. Russha just doesn't understand my stress. She gave me ALL this shocking news and told me I must change EVERYTHING I love in life. I know I can't make all these changes."

The client gives you many options here. You could focus on the statement about the client's stress. This stress seems to be a barrier, and if you do not know what the client is talking about, this might be a good area of focus. You could reply: "I want to make sure I fully understand the stress you are under; would you mind taking a few moments to help me make sure I know what is causing this stress?"

You could also focus on the relationship and communication with Dr. Russha. If there are concerns about how or what the client is communicating with the doctor, then this could be an area of focus, and you could respond: "It sounds like you don't feel Dr. Russha understands everything you are going through right now. I'm curious about what happened to make you feel this way."

You will want to know what news the client got from the doctor. This information could provide critical content that might need to be the focus of the session. To find out more, you could ask: "You mentioned that Dr. Russha gave you a lot of unwelcome news and this is bothering you. Would you mind sharing this news with me?"

This question starts with a complex reflection, since "bothering you" was not a part of the client's initial statement. The reflection then shifts to an open-ended question. Another way to decrease possible defensiveness is to ask permission from the client. "Would you mind sharing" gives the client permission to say no to the request. Asking permission gives the client a choice and power in the conversation, keeping the partnership strong and moving the discussion forward.

Let's say you have already talked to Dr. Russha or have an idea about the nature of the news. A question around the change statement might be an excellent opportunity to go mining for some change talk by saying: "Change is hard, and it sounds like you might have to consider some pretty important ones. How do you see these changes affecting your life?"

Here, you are avoiding the frustration with Dr. Russha and the last negative statement, "I know I can't make all these changes," and moving straight to the affect the changes will have on the client's life. This question might hit gold, helping the client to focus on actual changes in behaviors. Reflection on these possible changes allows the client's prefrontal cortex to contemplate their change cognitively. You could say: "It sounds like some of these changes are overwhelming. I'm wondering which changes that you feel you can succeed at right now."

Starting with the more challenging changes could just reinforce the feeling of being overwhelmed. Having the client talk about changes they could make during small periods of time builds self-confidence that could then be used to discuss some of the bigger changes later in the conversation.

Open-ended questions and statements give you a location to dig. The digging should be done as much as possible with reflections, affirmations, and the next skill, summaries, the *S* in OARS.

Summaries

The next OARS strategy is the use of summaries. Summaries are reflections that bring together several things the client has stated. A summary might be from just the current conversation, or it can bring together topics covered in previous discussions.

One of the most important roles for summaries is to help a client hear their ambivalence. Ambivalence is often unconscious; a person can describe their plan to lose weight while eating a donut, even if one of their action steps is to stop eating donuts (Miller & Rollnick, 2012). For a client who is motivated to improve their health one week, while the next week they focus on all the unhealthy foods they feel they can never give up, you could summarize: "Last session I remember you mentioning you want to improve your cholesterol level and better manage your diabetes."

Then follow this with information from the current conversation: "Today it seems like it might be more important to you to keep eating the foods you love."

This summary brings the conflict of sustain and change talk to the surface. Instead of continuing the conversation based on sustain talk, the client now can examine the conflict between their words and actions. This consideration will probably bring forth change talk that you can explore further through reflections and affirmations. Finally, summaries are an effective method for ending conversations or transitioning to other topics. They are great ways to end sessions on the same page as clients or to connect the current conversation to the next topic on the agenda (Miller & Rollnick, 2012).

OARS offer a set of skills that take time to master and integrate into your regular communication style. Here are a few suggestions to help integrate OARS:

- Try to decrease or eliminate closed-ended questions as much as possible.
- Focus on replacing questions with reflections.
- Increase use of affirmations.
- Replace typical responses like head nods, "uh huh," or other short verbal and nonverbal communications of understanding with simple reflections.
- Find opportunities to increase the use of complex reflections by adding meaning or feeling into your statement.
- End or transition conversations with summaries.

Over time, OARS will become your natural mode and the default communication style with clients.

KEY QUESTIONS FOR THE ENGAGING PROCESS

OARS skills are useful at many points in the change process and in interactions with clients. It's important to pay attention, though, to whether the client is really in the engage step or not. Here are some questions that can assist you in identifying when they are in the engage step:

- How comfortable is this person in talking to me?
- How supportive and helpful am I being?
- Do I understand this person's perspective and concerns?
- How comfortable do I feel in this conversation?
- Does this feel like a collaborative partnership?

A negative answer to any of these questions demonstrates the need for time to be spent building empathy and the helper-client partnership (Miller & Rollnick, 2012).

Next, we'll examine the role of trust and safety for engagement and ensuring that our approach is trauma-informed.

CHAPTER 7
TRUST AND SAFETY

The transformational processes of change and healing depend on our ability to create a relationship founded on trust and safety. Unfortunately, engaging clients with a history of trauma is a complicated task. Outcomes are dependent upon our ability to build a relationship with someone who often has little experience of what it means to be in a healthy relationship.

A healthy relationship has boundaries, expectations, and limits. These essential characteristics are not usually found in a relationship established by those with avoidant, anxious, and disorganized templates. Establishing a healthy, helping, relational structure with the client provides them with a new model for relationships that can translate into other aspects of life.

This chapter examines an important outcome and goal of engagement: trust and safety. Creating trust and safety is essential before moving on to the next MI process, which is focus. A client who trusts and feels safe with us is constructing a secure base. This base will be the starting point that will allow them to focus on difficult life changes and eventually find the motivation to act toward realizing that change.

We will start this chapter with an examination of why transferences make trust so difficult for many clients with traumatic pasts. Next, we will see how strategically building trust and safety opens the window of tolerance and allows hope to emerge. Finally, the chapter concludes with a look at concrete strategies that encourage trust and safety, while minimizing the chance that retraumatization and transference will occur.

TRANSFERENCE: HOPELESSNESS

Avoidant, anxious, and disorganized relational templates, past trauma, and intergenerational trauma all increase the likelihood that transference will negatively affect engagement. Transference occurs when the client projects his or her past experiences, and the emotions associated with that experience, onto the helping professional. The combination of their negative experience in relationships and the influential role that helpers play in clients' lives causes this to be a likely occurrence. While a natural part of the helping relationship, transference can negatively affect engagement if it is not identified and addressed appropriately (Wilson & Lindy, 1994).

One common manifestation of transference that can threaten the helping relationship is hopelessness. With hopelessness, the client puts the helper in the position of the savior. Interpersonal trauma is not only an abuse of power but also a failure of our society. The police did not come. A parent knew about the abuse but did nothing. The mental-health or justice system didn't take the abuser out of society in time to prevent the trauma. The client was powerless to prevent the event or situation themselves, and those with power were not able to or chose not to keep it from happening (Herman, 1997).

Then we enter their lives. At first, the client is likely to associate us with past authority figures in systems that failed them. But wait. You smile. You listen. You care. You say you can help with housing, food, employment, and other basic needs.

We play an influential role on two levels. First, we provide powerful psycho-social support in the form of empathy and compassion. For many clients, we are the only person in their life who values them enough to listen to what they say. Second, we hold resources connected directly to the client's basic survival and safety, such as housing, medical care, and food.

We offer a light of hope in a hopeless world. Helping the client see hope for a better future can lead the client to put unrealistic expectations on us. This transference is dangerous because all the client's dreams fall onto our shoulders. It's easy to find ourselves in the caretaking role, overstepping healthy boundaries and beginning to do everything for the client rather than empowering the client to do for themselves (Herman, 1997).

Due to the nature of the relationship, it's hard not to experience this type of transference at some point in the work with the client.

Taking on the role of caregiver is extremely detrimental to the partnership if we take a directing or authoritarian role in the change process. Successful change requires the client to be the one doing most the work. An effective way to know when you have entered the savior role is when it feels like you are working harder than the client.

When the savior dynamic occurs, it provides an opportunity to reflect this observation back to the client. A helping relationship is different than other relationships in the client's life. Revisiting expectations, roles, and boundaries keeps the client focused on the things that promote success.

TRANSFERENCE: TERROR

Many clients enter their relationships with us using an anxious, avoidant, or disorganized relationship template. This template serves as the unconscious foundation in which they initially view their relationship with us. Add to this the fact that most clients have been let down, bullied, and even abused by government bureaucracy, education, healthcare, and criminal justice systems that were supposed to help them in some way. When most clients begin their work with us, their brain is likely releasing the chemical dihydrotestosterone or DHT.

DHT, along with cortisol, is released when the client distrusts the helper or the larger systems in which services are being provided. It increases the likelihood that the client will be resistant or defensive, making it hard to stay inside their window of tolerance. Humans have a natural tendency to categorize people as friend or foe; in other words, we see people as trustworthy or as potential threats. Due to past abuse by others, the client, especially early on the relationship, may see the helper as a foe even though the helper's job is to assist them in some important way. The resulting DHT release can greatly compromise client engagement and improve the chances of transference (Restak, 2006).

For most clients, their trauma involved abuse by someone who had power over their lives. The abuser is often someone with a prominent role in their lives, such as a parent, police officer, partner, teacher, coach, classmate, or sibling. Abuse results when someone takes advantage of their physical, emotional, social, or economic power, and violates the dignity of another human being.

Authority and control used by the abuser result in the victim losing a sense of safety and control of themself and the world. In many ways, the helping relationship can mirror this power dynamic. We set the rules and are the gatekeepers to resources and services. The client, on the other hand, needs to follow our rules or risk losing access to vital resources and services. Most helping situations have some aspect of power disparity inherent to the structure of the relationship. This reality alone can increase the levels of DHT and cortisol in the client's system.

Power disparities between the client and the helper, coupled with the intense empathetic reality of the relationship, can often lead to the client transferring their feelings about their abuser onto us. The power differentiation and the intimate nature of the helping relationship will often trigger memories of the relationship with the abuser (Herman, 1997). This type of transference is unconscious and rooted in past traumatic experiences. Too often the terror transference results in retraumatization that often gets clients in trouble and even kicked out of programs.

TRUST

DHT and cortisol can lead to retraumatization, transference, and disengagement. All these traumatic responses make it difficult to engage clients in services and, even more so, around changing behavior. Luckily, there is a powerful tool to help reset this hyperaroused biology. While every helping relationship will have its difficulties, trust provides a foundation for safety, insight, hope, change, and healing. The definition of trust in *Connecting Paradigms* is twofold.

The first aspect of trust is an assured reliance on the character, ability, and strength of the helper. Our character and strength are a necessary component of building trust, and therefore our self-care is critical to the client's process of change and healing. If we are experiencing burnout or are struggling to engage in the work for whatever reason, clients are likely to recognize something is not quite right and put up relational barriers, which will negatively affect outcomes. Our ability to create trust with the client has as much to do with who we are as a person and being able to bring our best selves to the work as it is about our actions (Professional Quality of Life Elements Theory and Measurement, 2017; Lipsky & Burk, 2009).

Besides bringing our best self into the relationship with the client, we also must fulfill the responsibilities of our role; this is the second aspect of trust. Most helping relationships are a combination of work done by both the client and ourselves. We must not only fulfill the obligations of our role; we must ensure we carry out these tasks to the best of our abilities, delivering the highest quality possible. Many clients will expect to be let down, because this has been their experience in other systems and in past relationships; following through shows that their experience with you will be different (Wagner & Harter, 2006).

MI provides us with several road maps for establishing and maintaining trust with clients. First, the Spirit of MI (partnership, evocation, acceptance, and compassion), provides a set of strategic approaches to helping others that promotes trust. Second, OARS (open-ended questions/statements, affirmations, reflections, and summaries) helps us craft our communication style in a way that ensures our clients feel heard and respected. This builds the strength of the relationship. Third, avoiding the disengagement traps (assessment, premature focus, labeling, and chatting) helps us to approach our work in a way that encourages us to establish trust rather than damage it.

As we establish trust with the client, their biology shifts from releasing cortisol and DHT to releasing oxytocin. Oxytocin is crucial to bonding in any relationship. Oxytocin accounts for the good feeling we experience when we connect deeply with someone. Oxytocin increases a client's ability to stay in their window of tolerance, promoting flexibility, adaptability, cohesion, energy, and stability (Mate & Levine, 2010). Richard Restak (2006) provides a perfect summary of his findings concerning the chemical effects of DHT and oxytocin as trust builds in relationships:

> *Think of the experiments on trust as demonstrating the existence of two physiologic 'levers' in our brains (oxytocin and DHT) that activate in response to our interactions with other people. By creating an atmosphere of trust we enhance the oxytocin levels in the brains of those we come into contact with, and vice versa. Alternatively, if we signal distrustfulness, we activate the second 'lever' and increase DHT along with the accompanying likelihood of an aggressive response directed towards us.*

As trust builds, the client is better able to consider difficult and stressful changes and events for longer periods of time without falling into rigid or chaotic thinking. Oxytocin elicits feelings of contentment, calm, and safety. These feelings build a secure base, allowing for introspection and consideration about the harmful consequences of their current ways of thinking and behaving.

Trust is a two-way street. If we want the client's trust, we must trust the client and treat them with respect. It helps to understand that many client behaviors, even those that seem illogical and counterproductive, are at their core survival techniques. Trust, in this sense, means that we believe that the client is doing their best in the face of past and present challenges.

Next, let's look at the role of trust and oxytocin in eliciting hope.

HOPE

Without hope, the client sees no pathway out of pain and suffering. Without hope, the suffering and pain from trauma continue to dominate the person's life. Without hope, there is no motivation to address difficult change. You bring more than just your strength and wisdom to your relationships with clients; you also bring a mix of support and resources that elicit hope for a better future.

The research mentioned earlier showed us that hope, along with the quality of relationships and our techniques, drive outcomes more than any other indicators we can control (Murphy, 2008). In the last chapter, we saw how hope is one of the key predictors of engagement. Helping clients find a vision of a better future is central to the MI process and will be developed further in the next chapter.

The psychological phenomenon of the placebo effect demonstrates the biological experience of hope and why the relationship is so important. In the medical profession, an example of the placebo effect is when someone takes a sugar pill rather than an active medication, with the belief that they took the actual medication and will experience its therapeutic effects. Placebos create an expectation of improved health in the future. Hope, like a placebo, also creates anticipation of a future better than the present. Whether the person receives a sugar pill perceived to eliminate symptoms or sees the possibility of a better tomorrow, the body releases endorphins, creating a positive sense of the future (Mate & Levine, 2010).

Endorphins create an overall good feeling by reducing the

conscious experience of pain, increasing the sense of physical and mental well-being. Endorphins also relax muscles, improve immune functioning, and are shown to be a key driver of happiness. If the brain is lacking in endorphins, the result can cause depression and feelings of hopelessness (Cozolino, 2006). Also, when the client experiences hope or takes the placebo, they release dopamine and serotonin. Serotonin is like dopamine, which we discussed earlier. Both create a feeling of well-being and promote a sense of happiness (Southwick & Charney, 2012).

Here is where trust plays a critical role. Oxytocin makes endorphin systems more sensitive. Increased sensitivity acts like a kind of endorphin booster, which increases the positive physical and mental benefits of endorphins (Mate & Levine, 2010).

Let's return to the placebo effect and compare two situations to demonstrate the roles of trust and hope.

Situation 1: It is late on a Saturday night. You are walking home from a late dinner with friends. Out of the shadows of an alley, I emerge, having not showered for a week and wearing tattered and torn clothes. I approach you and hand you a bottle without a label and say in a slurred voice, "Hey, take these and all your pain will magically disappear!" You do not realize that I'm handing you a bottle of sugar pills.

Let's say that you are in an adventurous mood and the pain in your back has been annoying you all week. With lots of hesitation and a little worry, you take a couple of placebo pills. Here two biological reactions are occurring simultaneously. One is the hope that some of your pain will go away, which will probably release some endorphins into your body. The second is the nervousness about taking the pills and this person who emerged suddenly from an alley to give you free medication; this nervousness probably releases some amount of cortisol. You might get some psychosomatic benefits from my sugar pills, but due to a high level of uncertainty and the ineffectiveness of sugar to kill pain, we would expect limited therapeutic results in this situation.

Situation 2: It is 2 pm on a Tuesday afternoon. You are sitting in a medical clinic hoping to get treatment for back pain. You have already made an appointment and checked in. A nurse calls you back, takes your vitals, and does a quick initial interview about your medical issue.

Then I walk in. This time I've showered, shaved, ironed my pants, and am wearing a white medical coat with a name tag that says Matthew Bennett, M.D. I ask you specific medical questions concerning the level and nature of your pain. After several minutes of questioning, I provide you a diagnosis of arthritis and hand you a labeled bottle of pills with directions and a name you can't pronounce. I ask you to take two pills twice a day with food and state that you should start feeling pain relief in just a few days.

Again, you do not know that I just handed you a bottle of sugar pills. Because you want the pain to go away as soon as possible, you walk across the street to a gas station, get some water and an energy bar, and down your first dose. The biological release of endorphins will probably provide some immediate relief, the serotonin and dopamine will bring on a sense of contentment and satisfaction, and, since you had a positive interaction with Dr. Bennett, you will also have oxytocin to multiply the effects of the endorphin release.

These two situations offer the same solution to the problem, while creating two very different biological reactions. Clients entering services with negative experiences with professionals and systems will probably respond biologically in a similar way to that described in Situation 1 when discussing their future aspirations. Without trust and partnership, the client will probably view interactions with skepticism. As trust, partnership, and engagement build, the referrals and resources will be received in a more hopeful and motivating way, increasing the likelihood of successful outcomes and change.

The more one feels drawn by hope for a better tomorrow, the greater the motivation to take action toward realizing that future. The influence of this relationship can shift the chemical makeup of the client's brain from the pain and hurt of past traumatic experiences to one of hope and the possibility of a better future. Trust is also foundational for another critical aspect to change and healing, safety.

SAFETY

Without trust, there is no safety, and without safety, there is almost no chance for change and healing. For many clients, safety is elusive, as the dangers of domestic violence, addiction, homelessness, and lack of basic needs steal their ability to enjoy any real security in their lives. Without safety, the client will exist in survival mode and on the edge of their window of tolerance. The sense of being unsafe keeps clients stuck in rigid or chaotic thinking patterns, as they desperately try to establish as much safety and control as possible in their day-to-day lives.

Safety, in this context, is defined as freedom from hurt, injury, or loss. There are two types of safety you should consider when helping a client make a difficult change or to heal from past trauma. The first is physical safety.

In general, future thinking, goal setting, and prefrontal cortex functioning become difficult without physical safety and security. If a client must focus on food or shelter, this will dominate their attention. Similarly, an adult or child in a violent home or community situation will focus the vast majority of their energy into creating as much physical safety as possible, usually through rigid or chaotic thinking and actions (Bloom, 2000).

While possible, it is highly unlikely that someone experiencing homelessness, in abusive relationships, or hungry from lack of food will be able to make difficult change without a drastic adjustment in their living environment. Their situation will reinforce the epigenetic expression and resulting brain function that is helping them survive their dangerous present situation. We should focus all available resources on trying to help the client create physical safety. Only then will change and healing be possible.

The second type of safety is psychological safety. Psychological safety provides the client with confidence that you will respect their feelings and emotional well-being. This safety emerges from the trust we establish through our strength of character, consistent support, and follow-through. When clients feel comfortable being their true selves and disclosing fears, dreams, and struggles without worry about being judged, a secure base emerges. This secure base directly challenges unhealthy relational templates, building a client's self-worth and confidence to consider significant life changes (Bloom, 2006; Herman, 1997).

Establishing physical and psychological safety is a primary focus of trauma-informed care and is necessary for successful MI implementation. Without physical safety, there is little or no chance for meaningful change, as the client needs their brain and epigenetic expression to support survival functioning. Without emotional safety, clients will struggle to see hope or have the energy for insight beyond stress-based, rigid and chaotic thinking. While our resources and referrals improve physical safety, the spirit of partnership, compassion, and acceptance provides focus areas for building and maintaining psychological safety.

TRAUMA-INFORMED PRACTICES

Next, let's examine some trauma-informed practices that, if implemented, ensure high levels of physical and psychological safety. The goal is to eliminate potential triggers that may elicit transference, disengagement, and retraumatization, and to maximize opportunities to teach clients about what it means to be in healthy and safe relationships. Because the effect of trauma is unique to every client, no one can predict or eliminate all possible triggers, but these strategies help create safe relationships:

- See the environment through the client's eyes
- Ensure policies and procedures are trauma-informed
- Help set client expectations and boundaries of what their experience will be like in your program
- Build safety
- Slow down

See the Environment Through the Client's Eyes

One simple exercise is to walk through your organization attempting to see it through the client's eyes. Whether intentional or not, physical space, policies, procedures, and interactions with your co-workers and other clients all send powerful messages about the level of safety in the organization.

When you walk through the organization, notice whether the environment is safe, calm, and predictable, or whether it is overly chaotic or rigid. Do staff smile and greet clients in a friendly and welcoming way? The lives of many clients with unresolved trauma are a storm of homelessness, medical issues, drug abuse, and violence. Your organization needs to feel like a sanctuary from the storm.

Physical space and the body language of the staff are glimpses into the soul of an organization. Signs like KEEP OUT, STAFF ONLY, STAFF BATHROOM, or EXECUTIVE DIRECTOR PARKING ONLY send a clear "them versus us" message to clients, where we are likely to be seen as a foe. It is important to ask if the messages communicated are necessary. I'm not suggesting an organization should allow clients to roam their file room freely; however, locking the door is just as useful as a big KEEP OUT sign in red letters. Healing is a collaborative process, and the physical environment is a critical way to communicate that the organization values clients. A chaotic waiting room, signs creating the "them versus us" mindset, and a feeling of being unwelcome can all increase anxiety, reinforce negative views of self, and lead to disengagement (Bloom & Farragher, 2013).

Ensure Policies and Procedures Are Trauma-Informed

In addition to the physical space, many rules, policies, and procedures can devalue clients' sense of worth and lead to disengagement. The development of many policies and procedures may have resulted from a reaction to past intense situations that may have made staff feel unsafe. When we feel insecure or are outside our window of tolerance, we can become very rigid in our thinking. In the name of creating safety for ourselves, we might create overly harsh consequences or programmatic requirements that trend more toward traditional punitive models and fail to fulfill the Spirit of MI (Marlatt, Larimer, & Witkiewitz, 2012).

Even organizations with good intentions may unintentionally set practices and policies that dehumanize clients in the name of safety. As an organization takes steps to integrate the trauma-informed paradigm, it is important to reevaluate program rules and organizational policies and procedures to ask, "Why was this policy, procedure, or rule put in place?" Often no one will remember the reason behind the creation of a particular rule or behavioral policy. The goal is to review, in the context of what we now know about trauma and neurobiology, whether the policy is set up to help clients or if it is doing harm (Bloom & Farragher, 2013).

Some rules are designed to control behavior, and while these rules can be important, organizations need to be sure they first and foremost promote dignity and healing. Policies and procedures are critical statements about the values of the organization. Every operational policy should support the organization's goal of creating a healing, nurturing, and safe environment.

Help Set Client Expectations and Boundaries of What Their Experience Will be Like in Your Program

Most people have anxiety in new and unfamiliar situations. Add to this tension the fact that clients are entering a helping organization to deal with tough issues or past trauma, or that they may be forced into the helping situation by a court order or other external pressure, and this anxiety can easily result in retraumatization or disengagement. The better the client understands the expectations and processes of the program upon entry, the less likely they are to be retraumatized or pushed outside their window of tolerance.

An often-overlooked simple action is introducing the client to as many of the staff as possible. Throughout a client's time in the program, they might interact with several different people within the organization, from the front desk staff to billing personnel to other helpers. Introducing clients to as many people as possible sends the message that everyone is there to help them succeed. Many individuals with trauma histories have lived years without a community of support; the more people they meet in the organization who smile and welcome them, the more connected and safe they will feel.

As discussed above, every program has rules and expectations concerning client behavior, as well as consequences for those actions. It is important that clients understand these limits from the start of their time in the service. One of the most important expectations in a trauma-informed environment is creating shared expectations around professional boundaries.

Professional boundaries are expectations that set the foundation for a safe and healing relationship between the helper and the client. Clients with avoidant, anxious, or disorganized templates often have unhealthy and chaotic relationships. These relationships may lack limits or rules to keep themselves and others safe. To help model good relational dynamics, we must clearly state what clients can and cannot expect from us. Boundary setting should be done early in the relationship to set realistic expectations in the client's brain around the nature of the relationship.

Defining limits and expectations will require energy and dedicated time. It is important to ensure the client can also restate the boundaries back to us so we can make sure they fully understand. For many clients, the helping relationship might be the first relationship they enter with healthy boundaries and clear expectations (Herman, 1997).

These clients will have a learning curve with gains and setbacks as they get comfortable in this new type of relationship. We need to understand this and be as patient as possible as they adjust and start to feel safe with us, and be prepared to revisit boundaries throughout the relationship. Many clients feel overwhelmed early in the relationship and might not remember specifics of the boundaries conversation. Revisiting boundaries often reinforces their importance, while being sensitive to the fact that clients with severe trauma or elevated levels of stress often have memory issues resulting from the neurobiological effect of these situations.

Also, as the nature of the relationship evolves, you might find that different boundaries are being challenged by the client. The relationship might start to feel like a friendship to the client or they might misinterpret the intimacy of the relationship as romantic. These responses are natural when learning how to be in a healthy relationship and provide you with the opportunity to revisit boundaries in a caring and compassionate way.

While the client might unconsciously want a savior, caretaker, or some other role due to unhealthy relational templates and transference, having a conversation about clear boundaries will help them understand that this relationship is different. Once your role is known, it's important that the client also knows their role in the relationship.

Part of the discussion on boundaries concerns the client's responsibilities in the program. Many clients who live on the edge or outside the window of tolerance will struggle to remember even basic rules. Learning or following program rules might not be high on their priority list. It is important that we assist them in understanding the key expectations.

For some services, the only expectation of the client might be to show up on time for appointments. However, for many programs, the client has a set of responsibilities they must fulfill to get services and referrals. As with the helper's boundaries, it's important to have the client repeat what they heard and reassure them that we are there to provide support every step of the way.

It's also important that the client realizes they are responsible for their progress and success. As mentioned above, trauma survivors often long for someone else to take control of their lives. This transference might mirror past relationships where they were powerless, or could reflect their disempowered place in society. Make sure to state that their success in the program will be dependent on their efforts and not something magical you will do (Herman, 1997).

As mentioned above, stress and trauma can cause memory problems, and many clients will have difficulty remembering appointment dates, tasks, and other responsibilities (Cole et al., 2009). Make sure the program structures have realistic expectations based on your understanding of the neurobiological functioning of clients. When clients do not meet the expectation of the program, it might be a symptom of their traumatic past and not an intentional act of defiance. For program and client success, patience is critical.

Every program has rules and expectations concerning client behavior and consequences for those actions. Thoughtful use of disciplinary measures, with intentional feedback and an opportunity for dialogue, can help clients learn from their behavior and provide motivation for change. These situations can also be used as an opportunity to build new skills, rather than just be a chance to punish or sanction behavior.

Slow Down

The number one mistake we often make when working with clients with trauma histories is pushing them until they are outside their window of tolerance and a crisis results. Retraumatizing a client by pushing them too far and too fast damages the relationship and limits outcomes. Retraumatization occurs when we are out of sync with the stress level of our clients. Adding more stress can overwhelm the client's ability to remain on their high long road, which can lead to a fight, flight, or freeze response.

We are skilled at recognizing when a client's anxiety is rising. When we sense the client is leaving their window of tolerance, it's time to put our agenda aside for a few minutes to check in to see how the client is doing. Providing clients with time to talk about their emotions will lower their stress levels. Asking simple questions like, "Are you doing okay?" can help build trust and safety, while preventing stress from rising to crisis levels. Stopping to ask these questions can also provide an opportunity for the client to pause and reflect on their emotional state.

View the above practices as a checklist for aligning your organization's environment and client interactions with trauma-informed principles that promote safety. The goal is to work to eliminate potential triggers that can cause retraumatization, transference, and disengagement. Because every client and every trauma is different, you can't predict or remove every trigger, but there are strategies you can use that can help create an environment that promotes growth and reduces some triggers.

Helping others is a complex mix of the right support and resources. In addition to finding this mix for each client, you will see that clients need different things from us depending on where they are on their change journey. In the next chapter, we will examine how trust and safety help us focus the client's mind on their change in a way that promotes progress through the stages of change.

CHAPTER 8
MI PROCESS FOCUS

Each stage of change requires intense and sustained focus. Without focus, clients become stuck, not seeing or being able to take the next logical step. While focus is something that happens within the mind of the client, we play a critical role in helping clients find and maintain the focus that leads to powerful change.

The second MI process, focus, ensures that we meet the client where they are socially, emotionally, and in their stage of change. A mind affected by trauma and stress will struggle with emotional regulation and mental focus, and will need time to adapt and change. Trust and safety calms the mind and keeps the client in their window of tolerance, allowing the prefrontal cortex and the rational brain to consider strategically moving through the stages. Once the client is regulated and safe, we can help them to bring attention to the variables that will assist them to make a successful change.

In moving into focus, it remains important for us to keep strengthening the relationship, ensuring that psychological and physical safety increase, and avoiding the engagement traps (assessment, premature focus, labeling, and chatting). Focusing still relies heavily on OARS (open-ended questions/statements, affirmations, reflections, and summaries) as the primary communication strategy. Establishing focus with the client will assist them in identifying key areas that promote change and helping them move through the stages of change.

To create focus in MI, the helper and client work to develop a shared agenda. This shared agenda will guide the client's initial steps toward realizing their change. An effective shared agenda brings together the aspirations of the client, the expertise of the helper, and the resources and goals of the program to establish a set of common goals. Shared agendas formalize the helper-client partnership and set a direction that will guide the journey through the stages of change.

SHARED AGENDAS AND HARM REDUCTION

Too often, the requirements of the program or organization dictate the agenda, providing little room to customize services and resources around the unique needs of an individual client. Unfortunately, these demands can be reinforced by helpers who believe that one-way or a one-size-fits-all treatment approach works for every client, regardless of their history or current stage of change. This rigid method of delivering services leads to disengagement and poor outcomes. Luckily, harm reduction provides a different philosophical foundation for creating shared agendas.

At its core, harm reduction allows us and our programs to meet clients where they are in their journey to change. Harm reduction fits in comfortably with the other paradigms presented in this book, including MI and trauma-informed methods. Research continues to demonstrate that harm-reduction approaches have succeeded where traditional methods have struggled (Marlatt, Larimer, & Witkiewitz, 2012).

Traditional models of services often detract from focus and lead to disengagement. The moral model perceives behaviors as right or wrong, good or evil, punishing people who engage in these behaviors. The criminal model identifies certain actions as crimes. The disease model looks at certain behaviors as symptoms of a sickness. The cure for the disease often entails complete abstinence or eliminating the behavior entirely (Marlatt, Larimer, & Witkiewitz, 2012). As discussed earlier, trauma takes away a positive view of self. These programs can reinforce this thinking by adding additional negative labels or messages that clients easily internalize.

In contrast, harm reduction relies on compassionate pragmatism, which accepts that negative behaviors will always exist in society. This philosophy does not mean that we recognize every client action as right or ethical. Instead, we acknowledge that they exist and realize that the less damage they inflict, the better for both the client and the community (Roe, 2005).

Harm reduction is trauma-informed in that it challenges us to search for the deeper causes of harmful behavior. It goes beyond placing blame on the individual and identifies the social causes of the condition, which for most clients include big T and small t traumas.

This recognition of societal causes creates new possibilities for prevention and community interventions that not only address the client's struggles but the systematic causes leading to those struggles. Harm-reduction approaches, like trauma-informed methods, challenge us to shift the question from "What is wrong with you?" to "What happened to you?"

In harm-reduction, MI, and trauma-informed approaches, the problem does not define the person. While the behavior is harmful, the person has inherent value beyond their behaviors. Harm reduction allows us to meet the client where they are in their stage of change and does not put unrealistic restrictions on services. Instead, the helper collaborates with the client to set a shared agenda for services, because for lasting change to occur, the motivation for change must come from the client (Miller & Rollnick, 2012).

Compassion is limited in systems that see the client as immoral or sick. If, as a society, we believe the client's problems are caused by something that is wrong with them, and we do not acknowledge other societal factors and how past trauma is contributing to the situation, it is easy to place blame and point fingers, but that does not improve results. When the client internalizes this blame, it is even harder to find motivation for change and can lead to retraumatization and disengagement.

Structuring programs and delivery services based on harm reduction helps ensure that the Spirit of MI is at the center of our work. Harm reduction and MI have partnerships, compassion, and acceptance at their heart. Putting these two paradigms together creates a service atmosphere ideal for clients with traumatic histories to engage in their change and heal from past pain and suffering.

Harm reduction challenges society to prioritize the long-term best interests of the client and community. Giving a client who injects heroin clean needles might have a small upfront cost, but compared to the enormous cost of HIV or hepatitis treatment, the price of the clean needle is next to nothing. Needle exchange, free birth control, and other harm-reduction programs reduce long-term damage with less expensive and more effective interventions (World Health Organization, 2004; Miller & Rollnick, 2012).

Taking the view that a person is immoral or sick makes it easy to treat them as a person with little worth, which goes against the Spirit of MI. This attitude or belief leads to a directing and confrontational style of interaction that pays little attention to the expertise the client can bring to helping themself or their situation. Instead of resulting in the desired change, these interventions more often create resistance. In harm reduction and MI, the client is a partner with control of their services and treatment. This empowerment helps them see themselves as an expert with the answers necessary to improve their situation and well-being (Miller & Rollnick, 2012).

Few clients access services when their lives are running smoothly. Clients seek services when they are struggling with the consequences of negative behaviors and are coping with adverse life situations. Access to services is either high threshold or low threshold. Many traditional models apply the high-threshold model, where they ask clients to meet preconditions before they can access services. For example, to receive drug and alcohol treatment services, many programs require that clients maintain sobriety throughout treatment. This approach would be considered high-threshold access to services.

As with moral and disease models, harm-reduction programs often have abstinence as the end goal. The difference is that harm-reduction programs have a low-threshold approach to care. In low-threshold environments, we meet the client where they are in life and do not place behavioral requirements, like abstinence or other rigid conditions, on accessing services. This approach allows more people access to service, gives us a chance to start working with clients regardless of where they are in their change process, and works to stabilize and gradually reduce behaviors with potentially negative consequences. A low-threshold approach is designed to treat the whole person and not just one disorder or problem, setting the stage for high levels of empathy, compassion, and engagement (Marlatt, Larimer, & Witkiewitz, 2012).

Part of creating a shared agenda with the client is establishing how the goals of the program or organization guide your work and the services provided to the client. Harm reduction provides tools to help focus this work and maximize results. First, the helper has an awareness and understanding of the nature and causes of certain potentially harmful behaviors. This knowledge is a result of learning from the stories of the clients' lives and is supplemented by the helper's dedication to professional development.

Second, there is focus on enhancing coping skills to manage stressful situations. These can be frank and robust conversations surrounding behaviors with potentially negative consequences. It might be hard at first to discuss how to use an illegal substance or have sex in safer ways, but these are necessary steps to reducing harm for the client and community.

The third is the promotion of stabilization through training in reducing harm and increasing safety. The nature of potentially harmful behaviors is that they put the client in dangerous situations. Injecting drugs not only exposes the client to a hazardous substance, but it also might result in needle sharing and being vulnerable in unsafe social situations. In harm reduction, the focus is equally on increasing safety as it is on reducing present dangers.

Finally, we can help train the client in health-promoting behaviors. Many clients continue potentially harmful behaviors because the idea of abstinence seems too overwhelming. Even if the client has just one sober day a week, this might lead them to be confident enough to try two days a week. In another situation, a client who might not want to take medication for a chronic disease might be open to other healthy activities such as an improved diet or exercising (Marlatt, Larimer, & Witkiewitz, 2012).

Harm-reduction approaches engage clients where they are in the stage of change journey, keep us aligned with the Spirit of MI, increase the opportunity for change talk to occur, and increase engagement. They also serve as a foundation along with trauma-informed methods for clients to access our next topic, creating a shared agenda.

CREATING A SHARED AGENDA

Harm-reduction and trauma-informed approaches strengthen the helper-client relationship and deliver services in a way that helps the client's cognitive brain slowly gain control over emotions and survival reactions. Creating a shared agenda often occurs early in the helping relationship as part of establishing trust and safety. Shared agendas provide a destination and a rough road map for the change process. In creating an effective shared agenda, it is important to keep a few things in mind (Miller & Rollnick, 2012).

Shared agendas are distinct conversations that build upon the understanding established in the engagement process. They often entail giving up something or doing something new. In setting shared agendas, it is important for us to identify opportunities to shift the conversation from building engagement to focusing on creating a future direction. This shift usually happens when the client starts to move from the pre-contemplation stage to the contemplation or preparation stages.

Before making this shift, it is important to get permission from the client to advance the partnership. This agreement can be as simple as stating, "It seems like we've identified several possible goals for services. I wonder if you would be okay exploring these in greater depth?" Getting permission helps the client understand that the conversation is shifting into a more concrete and structured stage (Miller & Rollnick, 2012).

Once you have permission, the process of creating a shared agenda involves combining three areas: the agenda or goals of the client, the helper, and the setting. This approach continues to build the partnership while ensuring the consideration of all aspects of the client's change.

Shared agendas start with the client's desires, reasons, and needs for the change. The client's change talk provides a starting point and general direction for agenda setting. Understanding why the client is in services provides insight into their motivation. It is also important to help the client verbalize the future state or goals they are striving to achieve (Miller & Rollnick, 2012). If the client is struggling to verbalize this future desired state, you can ask, "Let's say everything goes perfectly for the next five years; what would this future look like?"

Next, it is important to understand the barriers to action. If the client could make the change on their own, it is unlikely that they would seek your services. Barriers can range from substance use to transportation issues to lack of system knowledge. Most clients will want a particular resource or type of support and have a reason they need you to achieve this goal. This desire is a natural starting place for creating a shared agenda (Miller & Rollnick, 2012).

It is important to continue to utilize OARS to ensure that the helper understands the emotional and tangible aspects of the change. Emotions stemming from high stress or past failures are often barriers to the change process. Here you can search for as much information as you can about the change and the affect that the current state is having on the client (Heath & Heath, 2010; Miller & Rollnick, 2012).

Stating your agenda is a critical step in building a true partnership. A partnership is a meeting of agendas. We bring our hopes and dreams for the client into the relationship, and it is important to state this outright. An example would be a provider of homeless services wanting all their clients to have permanent housing.

Even if the client did not bring up permanent housing, it is good to bring it up in the shared agenda process. Maybe the client doesn't know that you have access to this resource, or maybe there are other stresses in the client's life that did not lead them to put permanent housing on their initial agenda. Your agenda should build upon or supplement the client's desires, reasons, and need for change (Miller & Rollnick, 2012).

Shared agendas are great opportunities to communicate your caring and compassion. Statements like, "It is crucial to me that all my clients have the possibility for permanent housing" are powerful declarations of the helper's values. These statements communicate that this is more than a job and a paycheck for you and that you genuinely care about the client and their future (Miller & Rollnick, 2012).

Setting agendas are the goals of the program or funding source, which should align with harm-reduction principles, mentioned earlier in this chapter. Funding sources or federal/state programs have stated goals for the relationship, in the form of standards of care, requirements, or quality measures. These can be useful in defining the helping relationship, setting client expectations, and reinforcing professional boundaries. Every program has its rules, capacity, and limitations. While these do not always take the form of agendas, they do define how services are delivered (Miller & Rollnick, 2012).

Beware of the "them versus us" mindset. Many clients have had negative experiences in helping relationships in the past. It is natural for them to superimpose these experiences onto us before the establishment of trust and physiological safety. If the setting forces you into an assessment, premature focus, or label trap, you can explain that these are requirements of the setting and not part of your agenda. Here is an example, "Most of my clients hate this intake. Heck, I don't like it most of the time, but for you to get services, we have to get through it." Few clients will blame you if they know that it is a requirement of the setting (Miller & Rollnick, 2012).

RIGHTING REFLEX

Before moving on, let's take a moment to learn about a common MI mistake that can result in focus being replaced with resistance. The righting reflex is the desire to fix what is wrong with clients. For many people, this is the most challenging aspect of MI and can hinder all four processes. It is easy for us to think that we have the best solution and to impose that agenda on the client (Miller & Rollnick, 2012).

It is hard not to fix something when you know what the client needs to do. Having resources and services that can help a client address a painful situation makes it tempting to jump in and voice the need for change, instead of letting the client discover and hear their change talk. Even if you have the perfect resource or the ideal solution to the client's problem, that doesn't mean directing them to this solution will speed up the change process (Miller & Rollnick, 2012).

In fact, this act of "directing" is the number one cause of resistance. If a client is in the initial stages of change and you push your agenda, the client will probably stop focusing on their change and start arguing about their desire, reasons, and need to stay the same. The harder we push, the more likely the client is to dig in their heels and push back (Miller & Rollnick, 2012).

The righting reflex can derail the change process, even if it is grounded in the best of intentions. Luckily, MI gives us as a great skill to strategically avoid the righting reflex. Elicit–Provide–Elicit helps us to maximize engagement and focus while minimizing resistance.

ELICIT-PROVIDE-ELICIT

Up to this point we have primarily focused on ourselves as supportive partners in the change. In most helping relationships, you also fill the role of expert. The role of an expert helps to bring forth options and an increased focus on potential solutions. This expertise might relate to available resources, appropriate medical treatments, or other information that could improve the client's well-being. The Elicit–Provide–Elicit method gives structure to increase focus on change while maintaining the partnership (Miller & Rollnick, 2012).

The first step of the Elicit–Provide–Elicit approach is to *elicit* some initial information from the client. First, it is important to get the client's permission to provide expertise or advice. Asking permission alerts the client to a change in conversation, minimizing the possibility that the client will feel like we are lecturing to them. It also gives the client permission to state that they are not ready to move on to solutions. This hesitation does not happen often, but providing this opportunity empowers the client by giving them control, and avoids damaging the relationship by jumping ahead too fast. Asking for and obtaining permission maintains the partnership (Miller & Rollnick, 2012).

The next task is to explore what the client already knows about the subject. Exploring what the client already knows provides you with two essential pieces of insight. First, you can create your message around the client's existing knowledge. Many clients already know a great deal about their situation. Letting the client share their knowledge avoids wasting time on information they already know. Eliciting client knowledge also shows respect for the expertise the client brings to their situation (Miller & Rollnick, 2012).

Second, there is a lot of misinformation in society about medical conditions, services, and mental illness. When clients share their knowledge, you can address the misinformation and provide facts. If we jump right into providing information, we might miss opportunities to address misinformation, which can become a barrier later in the change process (Miller & Rollnick, 2012).

The final task in the first *elicit* is to measure the client's interest in the information that you can provide. If the client doesn't value your information, do not give it and do not take it personally. If there is a partnership established and you think something is important, most clients will be open to hearing what you want to share. Asking what aspects of a topic the client is interested in can assist you in shaping the message (Miller & Rollnick, 2012).

If there are multiple levels of information, ask the client to prioritize what they are most interested in hearing. Empowering them engages them from the beginning, and then you can save less interesting information for later in the conversation. Most of the time, all the information gets across; starting with what the client wants to hear increases the efficiency and effectiveness of your communication (Miller & Rollnick, 2012).

Here are some statements and examples you can use to

accomplish these tasks. To get permission, you can simply ask, "Would you be interested in some research I have on the effect of smoking on physical health?" or "Would you like to know about some great therapists in our area who work with survivors of domestic violence?" These questions put the client in the position of being an active partner in the process, and you avoid giving unwanted information that could harm the partnership.

To explore what the client knows about an issue, you can ask: "I'm curious; what do you know about the long-term effects of alcohol on the liver?" or "So I don't waste your time, I'm wondering what you already know about applying for Medicaid?"

To measure interest and help prioritize how to present the information to the client you could ask, "What would you most like to know about the resources available for your children?" or "Is there any information I can help you with concerning your Social Security application process?"

Once you have obtained the client's permission, explored the client's knowledge on the subject, and prioritized their interests, then you can *provide* your expertise and advice. In doing so, present information clearly and in small, manageable amounts. Most people can only remember a few key things from any conversation. Your task is to make sure that you present relevant information in small quantities so the client can retain and utilize this information for their change process.

Another critical task is to support autonomy and acknowledge that the client has the freedom to take your information or disregard it. The task here is not only to be okay with whether the client takes the advice, but also to communicate this freedom to the client (Miller & Rollnick, 2012). It's a powerful thing to say to a person, "It's your choice; no one can make it for you."

Next, let's look at a critical piece of information we *provide*: advice. Advice is a powerful type of information that can easily cross the line into the directing style. While MI allows for advice to be given, it's important that it's used sparingly and only with permission from the client (Miller & Rollnick, 2012).

It's also important to only give advice once the relationship is strong. There should already be a high level of engagement and an established shared agenda. If you provide advice before these two things are in place, it will cross the line from guiding to directing, possibly damaging the partnership, bringing forth resistance, and leading to disengagement (Miller & Rollnick, 2012).

A well-established tool in MI is the menu of options. The menu of options is a tool designed to give advice while promoting autonomy. All advice should be given in this format to avoid directing. Directing will often create resistance and even retraumatization. Offering a menu of options keeps the prefrontal cortex engaged in the conversation, as considering options is a cognitive process. Having choices concerning a difficult decision supports autonomy and helps the client stay in the window of tolerance (Miller & Rollnick, 2012).

Based on your expertise and experience, you help identify practical options for future action concerning the change. You then give at least three realistic options based on your conversations with the client. It's best to give the client the options that address (1) changing behavior and certain aspects of their life, (2) staying the same, or (3) somewhere in between the two (Miller & Rollnick, 2012).

For example, you could say, "It sounds like you are thinking about your drug use in a different light; it seems there are several options you could consider. You can detox and get into treatment, you can consider signing up for a methadone program, or you can continue your current level of use." Of course, the hope is that the client will choose the first option, but even if they decide to keep using, the relationship is kept intact, and you can move onto other harm-reduction strategies to increase the client's safety and well-being.

Avoiding the righting reflex with a menu of options is important. If you only give two options, there is a right answer and a wrong answer. For example, don't say, "You can stop using heroin, or you can keep using and eventually die." Even with three options, you need to make sure all three are real possibilities.

One last key to the menu of options is not to give too many choices. Most people can only consider three concepts against each other. Even four options can be too much for many people. It's better to give three and ask the client if they see any additional options that might work (Miller & Rollnick, 2012).

Whether providing advice or expertise, it's important to keep a few things in mind. First, make sure you offer it in small amounts with time to reflect. Too much advice or expertise is overwhelming and can lead to disengagement (Miller & Rollnick, 2012).

Second, acknowledge the freedom to disagree or ignore. This

freedom is a critical piece of communicating autonomy. If the client does not take your advice, it does not mean you failed (Miller & Rollnick, 2012). It only means that one path was explored and eliminated as a conceivable way forward. Statements like, "Sounds like this advice might not work for you. What thoughts do you have?" can lead to insight and build the partnership.

Third, it is important that advice is presented, especially in the menu-of-options format, as objectively as possible. We are invested in finding a way forward, but should be cautioned not to get personally invested in any path.

Next, let's look at the last step in the Elicit–Provide–Elicit approach, which returns to eliciting a response from the client.

The second *elicit* is a check-in to ensure understanding by the client and an opportunity to correct any misunderstandings (Miller & Rollnick, 2012). For more complex information, such as medical material, it's helpful to state, "We covered a lot today, and I want to make sure I explained it correctly. Would you mind telling me what you heard?"

Putting the success or failure on your ability to explain, and not the client's comprehension, gives the client permission to ask questions without feeling like they are not smart enough to understand the information. Make sure to take the time needed to clarify and answer any of the client's questions. Questions are often the way people process new information and how it relates to their specific situation.

Also, it is important to take the time to discuss the client's reaction to the information or advice. Questions like, "How does it feel to be sitting with this new information?" provide the client with an opportunity to check in emotionally with themselves. Doing this prevents negative feelings from becoming a barrier later when the client implements the advice (Miller & Rollnick, 2012).

Next, always do one last check-in to make sure the client can move forward with the information or advice. They might understand the need to take medication, but if they don't have transportation to the pharmacy, this might be hard to accomplish. Understanding the importance of change and implementing that change are two very different things. Utilize OARS to reflect any emotional reactions from the client. Even if the client doesn't verbalize their emotional response, it's important to bring any nonverbal cues to the client's attention. This reflection shows support, understanding that change is hard and most change requires giving up something the client enjoys or wants to continue (Miller & Rollnick, 2012).

Finally, end the interaction by supporting and affirming confidence in the client. You should assure the client that you are there to help if the client runs into any problems or issues. This last piece of positive support can make all the difference (Miller & Rollnick, 2012).

Elicit–Provide–Elicit is a powerful strategy that can help move a shared agenda forward. A focused client requires a focused helper. Working through the steps of Elicit–Provide–Elicit will take some time at first, but in the end, these steps will increase the likelihood of success.

KEY QUESTIONS FOR THE FOCUSING PROCESS

Let's look at some key questions you can ask yourself to see if adequate focus is established with the client. Negative answers to the following questions might indicate the need to create or revisit a shared agenda.

- Do I understand the client's future goals involving the change?
- Do I have different aspirations for change for this person?
- Are we working together with a common purpose?
- Does it feel like we are moving together, not in different directions?
- Do I have a clear sense of where we are going?
- Does this feel more like dancing or wrestling (Miller & Rollnick, 2012)?

Negative answers do not mean the helper has been unsuccessful. They only assist in identifying work that still needs to be done.

CHAPTER 9
MINDFULNESS

As the first part of *Connecting Paradigms* showed, the ability to focus is difficult for clients with a traumatic past or those struggling with small t trauma. Trauma demands that the brain strengthen survival functions at the expense of the prefrontal cortex, limiting the client's ability to consider, strategize, and plan around their change. Too often this biological condition keeps clients trapped in destructive habits, pain, and addiction.

The MI strategies presented in the last chapter will help clients focus in on critical parts of their change. Unfortunately, even the best MI practitioner will experience limited success if traumatized neurobiology persists. To help clients successfully focus on their change, we need to help them create brain states that bring them into their prefrontal cortex and allow them to strategically approach their change process.

Wouldn't it be nice if some supplement existed that clients could take to maximize their ability to contemplate their change and speed up the journey to change? What if this supplement also helped heal the biological and psychological damage done by trauma? And as a bonus, what if this supplement helped clients recover from addiction and other harmful habits?

The great news is that this supplement does exist. Even better news, it is free and is something each client has inside of them. Mindfulness is revolutionizing psychology and our understanding of healing. This chapter will introduce mindfulness as a tool that we can use to help clients along the stages of change and in their healing journey from trauma to post-traumatic growth.

DEFINING MINDFULNESS

For change and healing, mindfulness is a tool that strengthens the mind to the point where it gains the power to overcome the thought patterns and addictions of the biological brain. Recall our definition of the mind as a *biological, environmental, and relational emergent phenomenon that has the power to regulate the flow of energy and information*. Mindfulness activates and repairs the brain areas damaged by trauma, allowing the client's mind to exert will and volition over the unconscious brain.

Mindfulness strengthens the mind through the intentional act of focusing attention to consciously regulate energy and information toward healthier and more productive behaviors and ways of thinking. Without focused attention, the brain operates on unconscious autopilot. The mind reacts to things in the environment, choosing the easiest, most efficient course of action based on what the person has always done in the past, what brings the most pleasure, and what causes the least amount of pain.

The brain is amazing in its efficiency, but without mindfulness, it will repeat behaviors that might cause harm or are inappropriate for the situation. Focused attention is the act of choosing to be aware in the moment. Being present and paying attention to one's thinking and emotions allows the client to freely choose their next action.

Daniel Siegel (2011) offers one of the best descriptions of the power of mindful awareness:

> *With mindful awareness, the flow of energy and information that is our mind enters our conscious attention and we can both appreciate its contents and come to regulate its flow in a new way. Mindful awareness…actually involves more than just simply being aware: It involves being aware of aspects of the mind itself. Instead of being on automatic and mindless, mindfulness helps us awaken, and by reflecting on the mind we are enabled to make choices and thus change becomes possible.*

The research on mindfulness is evolving rapidly; every study documents new benefits from the use of focused attention. In a survey of the different approaches to mindfulness, researchers found five skills that are emerging as central to achieving the promise of this practice. Due to the state of their neurobiology, clients struggling with trauma might need months to master each skill. Remember, learning these skills requires most clients to build new structures in their brains to support this mastery while disconnecting many structures that have helped them survive years of pain and trauma. Although this process will take time, it is critical for clients making difficult life changes (Burdick, 2013; Davidson et al., 2003; Rock, 2009; Siegel, 2011).

FIVE SKILLS OF MINDFULNESS

In *Connecting Paradigms*, mindfulness is positioned as a set of competencies that can simultaneously heal the traumatized brain while building the ability to focus on change. In seeing mindfulness as a skill set, it takes away some of the mystery and stigma often associated with the practice. The five skills of mindfulness can be practiced and developed in two ways.

First, the five skills build upon each other in a uniform way and are applied to real-world situations. Mastery of a previous skill will provide the neurobiological strength to progress to the next. Each step might take weeks or months to master. While subsequent skills will strengthen before the previous one is mastered, this approach to mindfulness provides us with a road map for healing, focus, and improved outcomes.

Second, these skills apply to a client's mindfulness practice. Mindfulness practice is an intentional activity where the client is focusing their mind on a specific thing, such as their breathing, a prayer or mantra, doing an activity like walking, doing the dishes, a yoga stretch, or another intentional movement. The more the client practices mindful awareness activities, the more likely they are to use them successfully in real-world situations (Baer, Smith, Hopkins, Krietemeyer, & Toney, 2006).

Skill 1: Observing

The first skill is observing thoughts and feelings. When people practice mindfulness, they're attentive to the information flowing through their brain and body. Observing thoughts and feelings is a prefrontal cortex activity. This intentional act strengthens the high long road as it reinforces the synaptic connections that support strategic thinking and emotional regulation.

In real-world application, awareness lets clients focus on the choice in front of them. Without awareness, the client will unconsciously repeat past behaviors and habits without any conscious consideration of other possible choices. MI is only effective when a client can consciously consider a choice. Engaging in intentional mindfulness practices builds capacity to bring awareness to decisions that help the client realize their change.

Skill 2: Nonjudgment

The second skill is being nonjudgmental of the experience. Being abused, neglected, or treated poorly by another person tells the client that they are unworthy of love and dignity. Repeated trauma reinforces this message over time and leaves many clients with a sense of shame about themselves and their past. Too often I hear clients telling me that the abuse was their fault or that they deserved it in some way. While no outside observer would find any logic in this argument, it has become central to the client's personal narrative.

The second skill of mindfulness teaches clients to be kind to themselves and stop the harsh self-judgment. In mindfulness, we can introduce the concept that a client's thoughts and feelings do not define them as a person. Most clients will struggle with this at first; you should view being nonjudgmental as a skill that needs practice to fully develop. We need to work with the client to internalize that being nonjudgmental is about giving themselves permission to listen to what their brain is doing without passing judgment. Thoughts and emotions are transitory, passing things. They do not represent who the client is. It is very freeing when clients realize that their thoughts and emotions are not nearly as important as how they translate into action.

To build the skill of nonjudgment, have clients practice on less intense topics and situations. Have a client notice what people are wearing without judging it as good or bad. Challenge them to have a conversation without passing judgment on the other person; instead they should focus on just being present in the moment and paying attention to the other's words. These little steps will build the capacity to take on the harder task of applying nonjudgment to their thoughts, feelings, and behaviors.

Skill 3: Labeling

The third skill is labeling. Emotions lose their power when people assign words to them. The act of labeling emotions provides space for conscious consideration and a more rational reaction to what is going on in the environment.

Labeling is particularly challenging for clients whose Broca's area, responsible for language development, is damaged by trauma. Many clients act out because they are not able to verbally express their emotions. Being able to say, "I'm pissed off!", "Thinking about that makes me want to cry", and "I hate that person for how they abused me" is a powerful first step in gaining control over one's behaviors and breaking free of harmful behaviors.

Observing and being nonjudgmental provides the opportunity to practice labeling. Just as with the first two skills, labeling is a skill to be built over time. It is important that we understand that many clients will need a chance to develop the ability to put language to their experience as their prefrontal cortex and Broca's area heal over time. This labeling skill is one worth the time to build, as it will increase the client's ability to successfully engage in and maintain relationships associated with success in academic and employment settings, as well with relationships in their personal lives.

Skill 4: Nonreactivity

The capacity to label emotions allows clients to work on the fourth skill of nonreactivity. It is important to realize how difficult this can be for clients with a traumatic history. Reactivity has helped them survive highly stressful and traumatic situations. Their neurobiology has developed to support this responsiveness. Mastery of this skill requires that the mind has strengthened to the extent that it can override natural responses and triggers. Mindfulness strengthens the prefrontal cortex as well as the hippocampus, helping to calm the amygdala and keep the client in their window of tolerance, thus giving them control over their behaviors.

Traditionally, we have viewed inappropriate behaviors as something the client could control. Seeing these behaviors as choices might give us permission to punish clients for exhibiting them, but does not help the client gain control over future outbursts. Advances in neurobiology help show how challenging emotional regulation is for clients. If they are living in stressful or traumatic situations, we should have little expectation that their neurobiology can support nonreactivity without the proper support and time to practice nonreactivity and the skills supporting it.

Being aware that nonreactivity is the fourth skill helps us have empathy when we see reactive behaviors for clients still working on previous skills. It is a process to build competency for labeling emotions in time to not have a reactive behavioral response. Have patience through this learning curve, as mastery in nonreactivity will require changes in brain structure to support it.

Skill 5: Act with Awareness

The final skill, and the goal of mindfulness, is to act with awareness. It is here where clients can access free will and volition. With awareness, a client can consider their desire and reasons for change and start to envision a much different and better future. Mindfulness complements MI by providing a corresponding set of skills that builds and strengthens the brain areas and functions needed for adequate contemplation and action toward change.

BENEFITS OF MINDFULNESS

Research on the topic of mindfulness gained momentum once the realization of the life-changing power of the practice was fully grasped. Research demonstrates that mindfulness improves emotional, social, and cognitive intelligence. It repairs biology damaged by stress, trauma, aging, and addiction. Mindfulness increases the size of the window of tolerance, expanding the capacity for resilience and reducing the amount of cortisol in the body (Siegel, 2011).

Mindfulness has also been shown to increase the level of attunement with others and increases the quality of relationships in the client's life. Mindfulness practice can support engagement in services, as the client feels more connected and able to trust you and others wanting to help them. Mindfulness can also improve outcomes by addressing both harmful habits and mental-health issues. It increases the client's ability to quit or reduce substance abuse and other addictive behaviors while decreasing depression and anxiety.

Mindfulness improves immune functioning and facilitates faster healing from injury. Mindfulness might sound like a too-good-to-be-true miracle cure. Do not be misled; to realize these positive benefits, clients must practice and develop the skills of mindfulness over time. The outcomes help demonstrate why it is a journey worth taking (Burdick, 2013; Davidson et al., 2003; Langer, 2009; Rock, 2009).

Before moving on from the benefits of mindfulness, I want to add one more set of advantages to the list above. These benefits apply to you as a helper. I will argue below why it is important for us to practice mindfulness ourselves to help our clients, but for a moment, let's be selfish and see what we can gain from starting our own mindful practice.

Helpers who practice mindfulness have higher social, cognitive, and emotional intelligence. Mindfulness has also been shown to increase our ability to empathize with clients and bring compassion to our work. The combination of increased intelligence, empathy, and compassion allows us to be more attentive and attuned to what is going on with our clients. In other words, mindfulness helps us to build stronger and healthier relationships with clients, which we learned earlier was a significant driver of outcomes.

Mindfulness also helps us to decrease the stress that often leads to burnout and other negative consequences. We even feel more confident in our work, which is important when we are learning a new skill like MI. Finally, we also get all the benefits mentioned above that clients receive from practicing mindfulness (Davidson et al., 2003; Haidt, 2006).

INTRODUCING MINDFULNESS

Over the years, I have read a great deal on the science and practice of mindfulness. The research on mindfulness and its ability to repair the parts of the brain affected by trauma are some of the most powerful developments I have seen in my decades of work in the fields of psychology, social services, and public health. The word *mindfulness* never appeared in my course work during my three years of graduate work in psychology in the late 1990s. Today, mindfulness in its variety of forms is not only a driving force in psychology, but in our larger society as well.

While there is little doubt about the transformational power of mindfulness, introducing mindfulness practice can seem uncomfortable to many helpers, as it is vastly different from the standard helper-client interaction. As with any new paradigm, mindfulness challenges us to rethink the structure of client interactions. Here are a few strategies to help you introduce mindfulness into your work with clients.

Self-disclosure Strategy

Depending on your professional affiliation or approach, you may or may not disclose much about yourself and your life to your clients. Since mindfulness is such an experiential skill, I believe disclosing your experience around mindfulness is appropriate in most helping situations. I have found disclosure compelling, because if you practice mindfulness, it makes it less mysterious or odd for the client to consider establishing their practice.

I will disclose my experience here as an example for how I believe it helps to show the power of mindfulness and adds context to the research. I would start by getting permission and then move into the disclosure.

"I've been practicing something called mindfulness for a while now and have found it very useful. Do you mind if I share a little of this and see if it might be something you would like to explore more?"

Assuming the client says "yes," I continue.

"A few years back, I went to a training and heard about mindfulness. The trainer stated all the benefits people get from mindfulness, including decreased anxiety, less stress, better relationships, improved health, and better brain functioning. It got my attention, and I started to read more on the subject.

In the past, I had tried to meditate, but my mind was always spinning at what seemed like a million miles an hour, which made it hard to feel like I was getting any benefit from the practice. I would stop, then read another article supporting mindfulness, and try again. Then I read an article about how people who went through surgery have their wounds heal quicker when they practice mindfulness. That seemed cool, so I told myself I was going to try again and this time stick with it.

I started off simple. Before work, I would just take 100 deep breaths. As I exhaled, I would count off until I got to 100. After about a week I started to feel very peaceful and relaxed after about 85 breaths. The more I practiced, the fewer breaths it took me to get to this relaxed place. Soon I felt the feeling at 70 breaths, then 55, then 35, and eventually I spent most of my practice feeling a sense of calm and peace.

I was happy with this result, but it did not seem very practical until I was stressed out one day. I was running late for a meeting, and I hate being late. As I started to get increasingly stressed out, I instinctively took a deep breath. I could not believe how much better I felt. I realized I could bring that sense of calm and relaxation from my practice into my life by just taking a deep breath. Instead of speeding to my meeting and taking shortcuts, I just said to myself, 'Well, the world won't end if I'm ten minutes late.'

Mindfulness has been transformative in my life and has allowed me to control my stress instead of my stress controlling me. Would you be open to practicing a few of my favorite mindfulness activities?"

I have found that this simple disclosure allows me to demonstrate the real-world power of mindfulness and helps make clients more receptive to trying some practices in our meetings.

Teaching Neurobiology Strategy

I have found that clients connect to information about the brain and their neurobiology. Understanding how their amygdala and prefrontal cortex behave, with information about the window of tolerance, provides them with a context to view their struggles and reactions. Teaching the concepts presented in the first few chapters of this book have helped clients I have taught see that they are not bad people, but rather are struggling with biological consequences of past traumatic experiences.

The other reason I find teaching neurobiology to clients so important is that it provides a scientific understanding of mindfulness. I explain how when we intentionally focus on one activity, we force energy and information through the high long road. Each time we practice, we strengthen that road, giving us more power to maintain emotional regulation and bring our best self to the situation.

While it is possible to help clients practice mindfulness without an understanding of neurobiology, I have found a basic knowledge of the brain builds motivation to maintain a practice over time. In a world where we all struggle to find enough time, figuring out how to teach the basics of neurobiology might seem impossible. However, if you can find a few minutes, it can be life-changing.

Connect to Real-world Challenge Strategy

Another approach to building motivation toward establishing a mindful practice is to demonstrate how mindfulness can help a client address a real-world problem. Whether the client is struggling with stress, anxiety, addiction, relationship issues, depression, or illness, mindfulness can help them deal with those problems. Positioning mindfulness as a solution to a problem the client has stated can increase interest and curiosity.

Few clients will say "no" to the question, "I know you have been struggling with *insert issue*; I have some quick exercises that have worked for many of my clients. Do you mind if I explain a few of them?" Some clients might be ready to jump into practicing with you; others may benefit from your sharing your experience or learning more about mindfulness and the brain before practicing.

Practicing with the Client

Most clients will not be ready to go off and start mindful meditation for 20 minutes a day after utilizing one of the above strategies. However, almost all will be open to doing a short-guided practice with you. In an ideal world, all clients would be motivated to practice some form of mindful meditation every day; however, taking a few minutes to practice with you will probably be all they can manage at first.

Whether talking to a client who wants to dedicate time every day to practice, or one that is going to spend a few minutes practicing with you once a month, a few things are critical. For those with traumatic pasts, mindfulness can provide painful memories the space they need to enter the client's consciousness. It is important to give the client permission to stop if this does occur.

If memories do come to the surface, it can open the opportunity to talk about mental-health services, if the client is not already engaged. If you are the mental-health provider, it might open the door to process some of those memories. The main point you want to communicate is that if traumatic memories do come in, it is a sign to stop and process this with you or their mental-health provider.

The other important thing to communicate is what happens when less intense thoughts or feelings come up. I always normalize this experience by saying weird memories, thoughts, and emotions still pop into my mind even after years of mindful practice. These simple instructions help the client to get refocused.

- Notice the thought, memory, or feeling
- Accept without judgment
- Dismiss without engaging in the thought or feeling
- Return attention back to breathing (or other mindful activity)

I always like to add one more piece of research on mindfulness. Many of the benefits of mindfulness, especially those connected to healing the traumatized brain and building the capacity of the prefrontal cortex, are realized when we catch our minds wandering and bring it back into focus. This approach further strengthens the high long road. For most of us just starting a practice, struggling with focus is a positive thing, as it reinforces the logical and emotion-regulating pathways in the brain more powerfully than if we could easily focus from the beginning of our practice (Burdick, 2013).

The good thing about mindfulness is that there are a million different techniques that provide the outcomes listed above. There is a form of mindfulness for nearly every personality and mood; everything from yoga, mindful walking or running, loving kindness meditation, tai chi, guided meditations, and mindfulness video games can effectively help people achieve a mindful state. While it is beyond the scope of this book to go into detail on a range of strategies, I would suggest Debra Burdick's *Mindfulness Skills Workbook for Clinicians & Clients: 111 Tools, Techniques, Activities, & Worksheets* (Burdick, 2013) and Laurel Parnell's *Tapping In: A Step-by-Step Guide to Activating your Healing Resources Through Bilateral Stimulation* for practical tools (Parnell, 2008). If you do not want to rush out and buy another book, you can just search the internet for *mindfulness activities* or *brief mindfulness activities,* and you will have thousands of options to browse through to find one that fits your style.

Here is an easy example, just to demonstrate the simplicity of mindfulness practice. Have a client sit down; once they feel comfortable, have them close their eyes:

- Say "inhale", having the client inhale while you count to five silently.

- Say "exhale", having the client exhale while you count to ten silently.
- Repeat this for several minutes or as long as the client continues to feel comfortable and time permits.

This easy exercise is called 2:1 breathing. When we inhale, we prepare our body for action. The exhale has a calming effect. While you will be keeping count, have the client focus just on the breathing. As they breathe in, have them extend their stomach, pushing air into the lowest parts first and then working up to the chest. On the exhale, the belly comes in, forcing all the air out of the lungs. The client can put their hand on their stomach to feel what is called belly breathing and further support the feelings of relaxation and calm.

This example is one of my favorites for its simplicity and the fact that it brings together 2:1 breathing and belly breathing. You might find doing a yoga pose or some of the tapping activities in Parnell's book work better for some clients. The wonderful thing about practicing with the client is that you are both practicing, which sets a perfect stage for a great interaction once the exercise is complete.

For clients who are outside their window of tolerance and hyperaroused, even this short exercise might be difficult at first. Practice with the client during every session and have them practice once or twice a day for a few minutes. The goal would be to work up to longer times, but begin with a brief practice and build up from there.

MOTIVATIONAL INTERVIEWING AND MINDFULNESS

Simply, mindfulness is the practice of focused awareness. The neurobiology of trauma makes the focus required to move through the stages of change difficult. Besides strengthening the ability to focus, mindfulness also helps clients learn not to beat themselves up with every small or even large setback on the journey to change. Helping clients understand that they are not their thoughts or feelings, but being able to label those thoughts or feelings for just what they are will allow them to gain control over their actions, habits, and addictions.

Mindfulness and MI complement each other, as the outcome of mindfulness supports the goals of MI. There are few interventions with so much supporting research, as each alone can be transformational. Finding creative and innovative ways to integrate the two methods into work with clients can accelerate the change and healing process.

The awareness and focus we have discussed so far is critical to the next step of MI and is the subject of our next chapter: evoke.

CHAPTER 10
MI PROCESS EVOKE

Change comes from within the client. While outside factors such as safety and relationships play important roles in any change, the wisdom and motivation for successful action come from the client's life experience, resiliency, strength, and desire for a better future. In the third MI process, evoke, we help bring this wisdom and motivation to the surface so the client can hear their desire, reason, and need for change.

This chapter will introduce evoking concepts and skills you can implement. The next chapter, which focuses on mindsight, will bring together everything we have learned into a structured model to help clients gain insight and channel motivation into action. Like the engage and focus processes, evoke relies heavily on OARS (open-ended question/statements, affirmations, reflections, and summaries), and the engagement traps can still threaten the partnership. As you implement the skills put forth in the next couple of chapters, remember to always pay attention to maintaining and reinforcing the strength of your relationship with the client.

THE MOTIVATIONAL INTERVIEWING HILL

Miller and Rollnick (2012) provide the analogy of the MI hill to bring together change talk, MI skills, and the stages of change. On one side of the hill is preparatory change talk, which helps clients progress through the pre-contemplation and contemplation stages. In the hill analogy, preparatory change talk is the upward climb, which can be slow and arduous.

```
Preparatory Change Talk:              Mobilizing Change Talk:
Desire; Ability; Reasons; Need        Commitment; Activation; Taking Steps
```

(Pre-) Contemplation   Preparation   Action

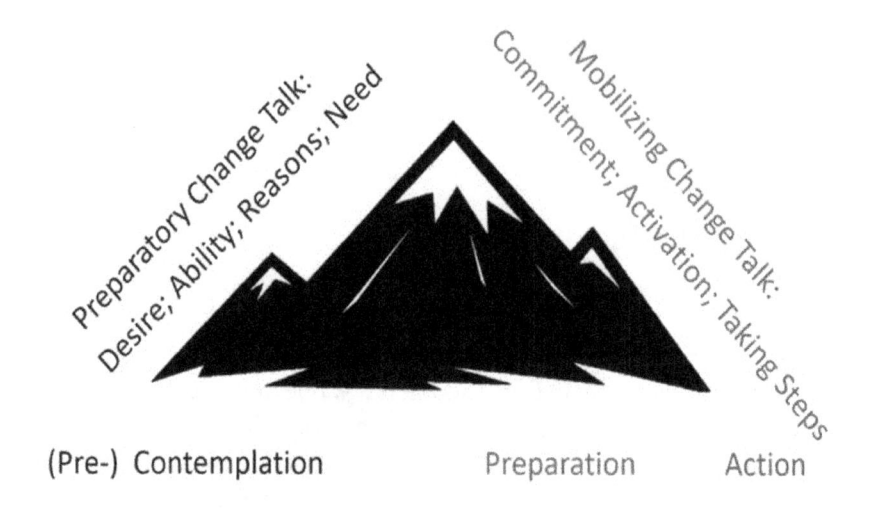

Figure 10-1: The MI Hill (Miller & Rollnick, 2012).

The journey up the preparatory change talk side of the hill is one built upon four key drivers of motivation. The more the client has the desire, ability, reason, and need for change, the further up the hill they will climb. A good portion of the remainder of this book will address how we can assist clients to identify and build momentum in these areas.

In any change, there is a tipping point. The desire, ability, reason, and need become significant enough to move from pre-contemplation to contemplation to the beginning of the preparation stage. The downward slope of the MI hill is termed mobilizing change talk. This side of the hill is about planning and action.

The strength of the client's commitment to the change will determine the speed at which they move down the MI hill. It also includes something called activation, which entails preparation and planning around the change. The pace of change on the downward slope increases with every action the client has taken toward the change; this is called taking steps (Miller & Rollnick, 2012).

Taken together, the acronym for preparatory and mobilizing change talk is DARN CATS. No one ever said that Miller and Rollnick lack a sense of humor! The rest of this book will help guide clients up and down the MI hill.

DARN: DESIRE, ABILITY, REASON, AND NEED

The DARN side of the MI hill is often rough and slow going, as the client fights through all the self-doubt and external barriers that have prevented them from making the change in the past. If you remember four words from this book years from now, I hope they are desire, ability, reason, and need. It is in DARN where the energy and thinking about the change come together to elicit motivation.

Desire is the extent to which the client wants the change to happen. Often, when a client is early in the change process, desire focuses on continuing old behaviors. Behaviors that are hard to change or stop altogether usually entail giving up something one likes to do. Drinking helps with stress. Taking a new medication may be undesirable because of side effects. Exercising every morning means getting up earlier. Leaving an abusive partner may mean facing danger and uncertainty. Ambivalence about change is natural and you should not push too quickly if the desire isn't there. There are other areas to research, including ability (Miller & Rollnick, 2012).

Ability is the client's self-perceived confidence to achieve the change. No one likes to fail. If clients do not think they can do something, they probably won't do it. We can assist the client by helping them identify past successes and strengths they might not have seen in themselves. As confidence and self-efficacy build, the chance the client will act increases. Believing one can change is a signal that change is possible (Miller & Rollnick, 2012).

Reason often comes from internal or external motivators, especially if there does not seem to be much desire for the change. Reason is the client's purpose for considering the change. For example, they may want to lose weight to address their heart disease or they may see they need to stop getting high because it violates their parole. A stated reason does not imply ability or desire. People are confronted all the time with reasons to eat better, exercise, stop using drugs, or get medical care. However, these reasons do not always lead to action (Miller & Rollnick, 2012).

Need is the importance and urgency the client feels concerning the change. An example might be that the client must stop using drugs right away or social services could take their child out of the home. Identifying need often involves external consequences that loom for the client if they don't make the change. While need can be a major motivator to preparation and action, it does not imply that the client has confidence in their ability or imply that there is a desire to make the change (Miller & Rollnick, 2012).

Preparatory change talk, like motivation itself, is dynamic. In one session, a client might talk about their internal desire and the external need to change, but they might lack the confidence or ability to take any action. At the next session, they might have more confidence, but the desire might seem to have disappeared, and the change might have lost some of its importance. This fluctuation is natural; the key to preparatory change talk is to spend time discussing wherever it lies on that day.

CATS: COMMITMENT, ACTIVATION, AND TAKING STEPS

While most of this chapter focuses on preparatory change talk, it's important for us to understand mobilizing change talk as well. The mobilizing change talk side of the MI hill helps the client move into preparation and action. For most clients, the movement from pre-contemplation to contemplation to preparation takes the greatest amount of time. Once over the hill, the transition from preparation to action usually happens more quickly. Let's examine what we can do to help clients move to the action stage.

Once desire, ability, reason, and need get the client up the hill, commitment becomes a primary focus. Commitment signals likelihood for action. If one person tells another they are committed to changing, the likelihood the change will happen just increased dramatically. If we hear the client talking about committing to an action, we should explore this thinking further (Miller & Rollnick, 2012).

Be aware that the client might not seem excited about moving to action. As discussed earlier, a challenging change is difficult because the client must give up something they love or do something they do not want to do. In addition to exploring the thinking behind commitment, it's important to understand the emotional effect of the change. In doing so, look for any positive emotions or excitement that might be mixed in with feelings of loss. Processing the emotional response will help keep the client inside their window of tolerance and from feeling overwhelmed by everything the change entails (Miller & Rollnick, 2012).

Activation indicates movement toward action, but also a lack of total commitment. Activation is often where our focus on planning helps the client to move from general statements to specifics. Planning in the MI context will be discussed in more detail in the MI Process Planning chapter (Miller & Rollnick, 2012).

Taking steps is the movement to action. Here, the client crosses from the preparation to the action stage of change. Taking steps often indicates that the client has already made some movement in the direction of the change. Think of this as testing the waters of what life would be like if the change happened fully. While these actions may only be the first step to a larger change, they are often the hardest to make. Many clients still struggle with self-confidence and loss as they move forward, so celebrate any achievements, no matter how small (Miller & Rollnick, 2012).

The rest of this chapter will present strategies to help the client journey up the MI hill by evoking preparatory change talk. It will examine methods to help clients bring forth their desire, ability, reason, and need in a way that can facilitate conversations about their change. First, let's look at how to elicit change talk specifically concerning ability.

ABILITY STRATEGIES

For change to happen, there must be hope or the belief that change is possible. Ability is when the client believes they have skills and resources to make change happen. Combine the two and self-efficacy emerges. Self-efficacy is the belief that change is possible and that the client knows they can contribute to making it happen (Bandura, 1988).

Without hope, the client will stay stuck at the bottom of the MI hill. Hope gets them to the base of the hill, ability gives them the tools to climb, and self-efficacy provides the emotional and intellectual motivation to take the first step. The desire, reason, and need are still necessary to push the client up the hill, but without hope and self-efficacy, they will often not have the courage to take the first step.

A good way to develop the power of hope, ability, and self-efficacy is to help the client establish what is known as a growth mindset. Carol Dweck (2006) has conducted some amazing research on an expression of self-confidence she calls the growth mindset. Dweck explains the concept in the following way:

> *This growth mindset is based on the belief that your basic qualities are things you can cultivate through your efforts. Although people may differ in every which way... [people with a growth mindset] believe that a person's true potential is unknown (and unknowable); that it's impossible to foresee what can be accomplished with years of passion, toil, and training.*

Past experiences, both struggles and successes, affect how a client views themselves. These views fall into either growth mindsets or what Dweck calls fixed mindsets. Growth mindsets build confidence in one's ability. Fixed mindsets create artificial limits as to what the client can accomplish. Shifting from fixed to growth thinking increases self-confidence and helps the client shake off the victim mindset often associated with traumatic experiences (Dweck, 2006).

The victim mindset is a natural consequence of trauma. Everyone who is traumatized is a victim of something or someone. In the victim mindset, the trauma has power over the client and keeps them stuck in the pain and suffering associated with the trauma. The victim has a negative view of themselves in the world. A fixed mindset is often a consequence of not being able to recover and get out of the pain and suffering caused by big T or small t trauma.

Helping clients develop their growth mindset is a critical part of transforming pain and suffering into strength and wisdom. During this transformation, the client sheds the victim thinking and starts to see themselves as a survivor who is no longer a prisoner of their past pain. The trauma's grip loosens and a new person emerges. As this transformation happens, you should hear more growth mindset language emerge. You can support this emergence through affirmations and helping the client identify any residual fixed-mindset thinking that might still be holding them back.

Clients struggling with fixed mindsets focus on being judged. This often manifests as feelings of shame about what happened to them or actions they are not proud of in their past. As mentioned earlier, trauma can make clients feel worthless; in the fixed mindset, this comes out as a constant sense that everyone is judging them (Dweck, 2006).

Stuck in fixed thinking, clients fail to assert growth mindsets, which allow clients to search for areas to improve. Trauma and fixed mindsets prevent clients from seeing possible ways to improve their situation. If they do not think they can make their lives better, opportunities that might seem obvious to us might not seem like viable options to clients. Fixed thinking is often combined with the reality that many clients are focused on surviving their current impoverished or dangerous situation, making future thinking that much more inaccessible.

Trauma, past failures, and current struggles make growth thinking difficult. However, our society often promotes fixed thinking without understanding the consequences. One of the strategies many well-meaning parents use to boost their children's self-esteem is to say statements like: "You're a natural at science" or "You are so smart." Pay attention to the language being used here, because it's critical. Messages like this become integrated into the child's personality. Success or failure in the fixed mindset becomes about talent or personality and not effort expended.

In contrast, growth mindset statements like, "You worked so hard for that A on your chemistry test" or "You've really put a lot of effort into your homework this year and look how your grades have improved" equate success with effort and variables the person has control over.

So, why is this important? Well, if a child believes they're great in science and then gets a D on a chemistry test, they'll internalize this as, "I'm a failure." Dweck found that this led to feelings of depression or anxiety in the face of stressful situations. If they think, at their core, they're now "bad" at science, it destroys motivation to work harder next time because the outcome is disconnected from the level of effort (Dweck, 2006).

Many clients continue to struggle with this language throughout their life. As mentioned earlier, we too often put label after label on our clients. Homeless, mentally ill, HIV-positive, offender, or criminal are not labels our society makes easy to shed. Too often clients internalize these labels and can't see a life without them. Moving from a fixed to a growth mindset entails helping clients see that their struggles are conditional and not who they are as people.

In contrast, a client with a growth mindset realizes that success is a result of the effort put forth. If confronted with hardship or setbacks, the growth mindset motivates the client to work much harder and not give up. They recognize that there's the possibility of a better future. A growth mindset means knowing that a better tomorrow is dependent on the effort and work invested in making it a reality (Dweck, 2006).

Those with a fixed mindset believe that some people are born superior. Natural talent may help some people succeed in things like music and sports, but Dweck's research shows that successful people, even world-class musicians and athletes, work harder to develop their talents. Few geniuses are born. Instead, genius comes out of hours, days, years, and decades of dedication and practice. Those who believe their skills are a result of arduous work spend more time developing these skills and expertise (Dweck, 2006).

The fixed mindset results in missed opportunities for growth. A challenge shuts down any motivation to improve one's situation. On the other hand, a challenge motivates those with a growth mindset to work with great resiliency and robustness when confronted with an initial setback (Dweck, 2006).

Helping shift a client's self-talk from a fixed mindset to a growth mindset takes time and repetition. This change is critical to building confidence in one's ability to accomplish their change. In the last chapter, we learned mindfulness practice and skill building will help the client learn to be nonjudgmental; mindfulness will also complement the client's ability to hear their fixed mindset and replace it with a growth mindset. Here are some additional steps you can use to help clients shift from a growth to fixed mindset.

The first step in changing a fixed mindset into a growth mindset involves helping the client to hear their fixed mindset voice. To understand and implement this reframe, it is important to provide a little information about fixed and growth mindsets. You can talk to the client about the brain being a muscle; the more you use the areas that promote confidence and resiliency, the stronger those areas will become. In contrast, the more they put themselves down or speak negatively of their ability, the muscle that prevents action will become stronger and stand as a greater obstacle for change.

You could also use the path to superhighway analogy we explained in earlier chapters of this book in our discussion about synaptic strength and efficiency. The important thing to help the client realize is that their own self-talk will determine their ability to be successful in their change. Since many clients' views of themselves are negative, approach this gently, using the steps presented in the mindfulness chapter.

- Notice the thought, memory, or feeling

- Accept without judgment
- Dismiss without engaging in the thought or feeling

The next step is for the client to recognize that they have a choice. The key here is that the client has an option to develop a skill or not; they can put forth the effort or put their energy somewhere else. People are not slaves to their past failure; they are products of their focus and energy.

Once the client shifts their thinking from a fixed to a growth mindset, it's usually a call to action. As self-efficacy increases, motivation builds into energy for action. The client will still need help finding the desire, need, and reason for traveling up the MI hill, but shifting from a fixed to a growth mindset will provide both hope and the energy necessary to take the first step toward change.

There are some additional questions that elicit preparatory change talk specifically to develop the client's confidence in their ability. If a client is struggling to see any hope or find the confidence needed for action, try a question like: "What were things like before you started using drugs?"

This type of question helps connect the client back to a better time. If they struggle to find confidence in the person they are now, they might see that they did have strengths in the past that they could use to make the change happen.

Many of our clients have been through a lot in their lives, and their current challenge is one in a long line of struggles they have survived. Another question that can help them find strength is: "What changes have you made in your life that were difficult for you? How did you do it?"

If they can identify one change, this will directly elicit talk about ability. Use OARS to explore past success in detail. Talking about ability builds self-efficacy.

Like the last question, asking, "Given what you know about yourself, how could you make this change successfully?" gets the client thinking about their ability and strengths.

Finally, a more direct way to measure self-confidence, especially if the client has expressed some hope around their change, is to ask: "What gives you some confidence that you can do this?" This question reinforces the strengths the client sees in themselves.

As you ask these ability-eliciting questions, it is appropriate to bring up any strengths you see in the client. Start with what the client can see in themselves, and build their confidence with accomplishments you witnessed them achieve in the past, or strengths you can identify through your work together. The client's knowledge that someone else sees strengths in them can be a critical piece to building self-efficacy and motivation.

THE IMPORTANCE/CONFIDENCE RULER

The importance/confidence ruler is a simple yet powerful MI tool that both addresses ability as well as desire, reason, and need. There are three goals that the importance ruler helps accomplish. First, it can be utilized to elicit preparatory change talk through the asking of scaling questions and follow-up conversation. Next, it can be used to increase the importance the change holds for the client. Finally, it can be utilized to enhance the client's self-confidence in their ability to make the change (Miller & Rollnick, 2012).

The importance-ruler strategy consists of two scaling questions that can easily integrate into most conversations with clients. The first question measures the level of desire, reason, and need: "On a scale from 1 to 10, with 1 as not important at all and 10 as extremely important, how important is it for you to change?" The second question measures the level of confidence the client has in their ability to make the change: "On a scale from 1 to 10, with 1 as not confident at all and 10 as extremely confident, how confident are you that you could make this change?" (Miller & Rollnick, 2012).

The answer the client gives is not nearly as important as the opportunity the answer provides for change talk. The follow-up questions are where the magic of the importance ruler happens. It's almost impossible not to elicit some change talk through this process.

Let's say you asked the client, "On a scale from 1 to 10, with 1 as not confident at all and 10 as extremely confident, how confident are you that you could quit smoking?" and the client responded with "3."

There are two ways of working with this low number. The first response could be "Why are you at a 3 and not a 1?" Even though a 3 is not very high, asking why the client isn't at a lower number elicits talk about the confidence the client does possess when it comes to quitting smoking. For answers ranging from 2 to 5, this follow-up is highly effective, as the client is speaking to what has motivated them to this point. While their low score shows there is work to be done before action occurs, asking why they are not at a lower number will provide you plenty of positive change talk to explore (Miller & Rollnick, 2012).

Another approach is to ask, "What would it take for you to go up one point from a 3 to a 4?" The first question focused on work already done by the client. This question focuses on what work would need to be done to move up the MI hill. This works well with answers of 1 or answers above 5. For 1s, you should follow up with "What would it take for you to go from a 1 to, say, a 2 or maybe a 3." Clients at 1 probably cannot see beyond the next small step, so having them think about being a 5 or 6 may be out of reach.

Clients with answers of 6 or above are showing a higher level of desire, ability, reason, or need, so they can be pushed a little more. If a client says they are a 7, you could follow up with, "What would it take for you to go from a 7 to, say, a 9 or even a 10?" In their answer, the client will probably talk about their last barriers to change, as well as positive actions they could take to overcome those barriers.

Many helpers who utilize MI incorporate the importance-ruler scaling questions into intakes, interviews, and assessments. This integration opens opportunities to explore change right from the start of the relationship. Asking the scaling questions during intake also gets the client used to being asked these types of questions, giving you and the client a baseline to work from throughout the relationship.

It might also be useful to integrate the answers to the scaling questions into formal treatment or service plans. Combining them into established planning processes provides a trigger to reevaluate. Each time the questions are asked, you elicit change talk. The hope is that the numbers trend in a positive direction over time, but again, the most important thing is the elicitation of change talk.

Importance- or confidence-ruler questions are easily incorporated into every visit. Start a change discussion by asking, "Last time we met, we talked about the importance of you getting into medical care. You stated that you were at a 4. I wonder if that number has changed at all?" Regardless of the answer, you now have set the focus of the meeting and can ask one of the follow-up questions. The answer will also help you identify whether the client has progressed or regressed in their stage of change. Integrating the importance ruler into the structures of the helping relationship is a pragmatic way to incorporate MI into the day-to-day work with clients, thus improving the effectiveness of conversations about change.

In the next chapter, on mindsight, we will revisit the role of the importance ruler in helping clients gain a deep level of insight into their situations. Next, let's look at some additional methods to elicit talk around desire, reason, and need.

DESIRE, REASON, AND NEED STRATEGIES

In MI, the confrontation is not with someone else, but with one's self. (Miller & Rollnick, 2012)

There might be outside pressures on the client to change, but these often only elicit resistance if we put too much focus on them. In MI, you assist the client to internalize the difference between the present situation and the life the client wants to live.

One strategy to elicit change talk around desire, ability, and need is to agree with a twist. This strategy is effective when the conversation is dominated by the client's sustain talk. These are powerful statements that take some practice and are only utilized when there is no change talk to explore (Miller & Rollnick, 2012).

The premise behind agreeing with a twist is that it's hard for the client to argue with you when you agree with them. This is a way to have the feedback reach the prefrontal cortex while keeping them in their window of tolerance. You are not challenging the client, but providing a complex reflection, tying the sustain talk to the client's sense of self.

Here are a couple of examples. A client is discussing their drinking habits. If the client is just giving you reasons they will keep drinking, you could state: "Drinking seems like a very important part of your life, and it seems you would lose a lot if you stopped." Again, this is a complex reflection, so do not use this statement unless the client has been injecting a good deal of sustain talk into the conversation.

Another agreement with a twist for this situation could be: "You just wouldn't be you without a beer in your hand. It's so important that you may just have to keep on drinking no matter the cost." Most people have a strong reaction to being connected to their behaviors in this way and will argue back that drinking is not that important. Of course, this argument is all change talk for client and you to explore further.

Another strategy that can help to find change talk, even when it seems there is little coming from the client, is to ask about extreme or future consequences. This is an excellent way to shift the conversation away from sustain talk toward the reason and need for change. An example of this approach is to ask, "Tell me the worst thing that can happen 10 years from now if your blood pressure stays at its current level." Instead of your making the argument for change, the client must come face to face with the consequences of their behavior coming out of their own mouth and not yours. This statement directly elicits reason and need for the client to consider the change, and is also a way for you to stay out of the expert and advice-giving role (Miller & Rollnick, 2012).

You can also put a positive spin on the future consequence question. An example is: "If you decide to make this change, what do you hope will be different in the future?" This positive spin also elicits reason and need, while opening the door for the client to talk about their desire to have a different outcome.

A similar statement, "If everything goes perfectly the next five years, tell me what your life would look like," helps bring forth the client's hopes and dreams for the future. Many clients with traumatic histories might not be able to see far into the future. This inability to project hope into their future is disheartening, but provides us with critical information. If a client is unable to visualize a year or two into the future, we want to make sure our statements target very short-term changes. Over time we can help them build a better vision for their future.

The next strategy, the decisional balance sheet, has fallen out of favor in the 3rd edition of the MI book. However, it has been a popular strategy in the past, so it's at least worth a mention here. The decisional balance sheet is a pros and cons list, answering the questions, "What are the negative costs of making this change?" and "What are the benefits of making this change?"

Decisional balance sheets have fallen out of favor because the exercise directly elicits sustain talk through the creation of a list of cons. Having someone discuss why they love drinking makes the synapses in the brain that support the habit go wild. Once this happens, it is hard to maximize the effect of the list of pros (Miller & Rollnick, 2012).

Decisional balance sheets can still be of use when you do not want to promote change in a direction. Let's say a client is considering breaking up with a boyfriend. The helper is neutral about the client's boyfriend, knowing the client might be able to find someone a little more nurturing and supportive, but also remembering the client has been in much worse relationships in the past.

The decisional balance sheet can be used as a last resort if all other attempts have failed to elicit any change talk. If the client is going to go on and on about why they're not going to change, the decisional balance sheet does force contemplation on change, and therefore can still be useful.

Hearing one's change talk is a powerful moment in the change process. One's own voice making the argument for change is often the crucial moment when a client moves from pre-contemplation to contemplation. It is the moment when the client realizes that they do deserve a better life than the one they are currently living.

To this point, we have learned how to build the relationships, help clients focus attention on a change, and give clients the opportunity to hear change talk coming out in their words. In the next chapter, we will bring all these concepts together in a structure called mindsight.

CHAPTER 11
MINDSIGHT

Mindsight is a word termed by Daniel Siegel (2011) to describe utilizing mindful awareness to apprehend the inner nature of things and see them intuitively. Mindsight is the deep level of insight that is connected to who we want to be as people and what we aspire to in our lives. Whereas insight might help one see a problem in a different light, mindsight is insight with the motivation needed to transform oneself and one's life.

In this chapter, we will present the five steps of mindsight and how you can use them to help focus a client on their desire, ability, reason, and need for change, while evoking their wisdom and experience. These steps are mindfulness, identifying ambivalence, cognitive dissonance, hope and self-efficacy, and motivation. To make this chapter come to life, think about a change you would like to make in your own life. Choosing a change where you are in the contemplation or preparation stage would be most helpful for our example.

Let's start by using the importance ruler to measure your confidence and how much importance you assign to your change. Please write down the answers to the following:

- *On a scale of 1 to 10 (1 being not at all important and 10 being extremely important), how important is it for you to change?*
- *On a scale of 1 to 10 (1 being not at all confident and 10 being extremely confident), how confident are you that you can make this change?*

STEP 1: MINDFULNESS

Mindsight relies on the client's ability to consider that their life is not aligned with their values. This difficult and intense process requires a great deal of emotional regulation, internal reflection, and situational awareness. Change involves stress; without mindfulness, the stress associated with a change can push a client outside their window of tolerance and hurt engagement.

Stress that leads to a positive action is termed eustress (Siebert, 2005). Eustress drives us to show up on time for work, be the best parent possible for our children, and do things to improve ourselves personally and professionally, such as reading this book! Mindsight requires a type of eustress called cognitive dissonance, which occurs when the client realizes that they are not living a life that aligns with their values. This type of stress is positive, in that it provides the motivation for action to rectify the situation.

While eustress results in positive action, it often pushes clients to the edge of their window of tolerance. Mindfulness helps clients to experience this stress without becoming reactive. As mentioned in the chapter on mindfulness, it would be ideal if all clients were engaging in mindfulness practices every day. Knowing that is not always the reality, practicing with the client before having a mindsight conversation and giving them coping skills to utilize, like deep breathing if they feel they are getting stressed, can increase their capacity for internal reflection.

STEP 2: IDENTIFYING AMBIVALENCE

Ambivalence is wanting more than one thing at the same time when those things are incompatible, and has been mentioned several times throughout this book. Ambivalence keeps us locked into harmful behaviors or habits. The step of identifying types of ambivalence provides us with a foundation to guide our reflections and summaries. Insight into ambivalence assists us in establishing the shared agenda and the planning discussed in the next chapter.

The first type of ambivalence is approach/approach. This ambivalence occurs when a client struggles with two choices that both have positive outcomes. Considering one choice accentuates the attractiveness of the other and vice versa. While approach/approach can delay decision making, it is usually the least stressful form of ambivalence (Miller & Rollnick, 2012).

You are at your favorite restaurant. The waiter is reading off the specials, and your mouth starts to water when he mentions that the filet mignon is on special. But wait, in the next moment, before you can say yes, he describes the fresh tuna that is also on special, your favorite fish!

You start to say the word "tuna," but you see the table next to you getting their filets and they look amazing. Just as you are about to say, "the steak special," you recall the amazing tuna you had a few months before at this restaurant as one of the best meals of your life. What choice will you make?

In defining approach/approach, you have probably realized that this is not the form of ambivalence that keeps most clients stuck in the contemplation stage. Choosing between two great colleges, which new restaurant to go to for lunch, or whether to play tennis or golf are not even thoughts in most clients' minds. On occasion, someone on the downslope of the MI hill might have some approach/approach ambivalence, which usually means you have done a lot of great work together up to that point and they are moments away from entering the action stage (Miller & Rollnick, 2012).

The second type of ambivalence is avoidance/avoidance and is much more common in helping relationships. Here the choice is between two unpleasant alternatives. This type is the old situation of being stuck between a rock and a hard place. As the client moves toward making a decision in one direction, the negatives of the choice become clearer, and the alternative might begin to look more favorable. Unfortunately, as soon as they move toward the alternative, the negatives of that choice come into focus (Miller & Rollnick, 2012).

A client experiencing homelessness might be trying to consider whether to sleep under the bridge or go to the shelter. He had a terrible experience in the shelter last week and did not like it there. However, it is supposed to be to be cold the next couple of nights, so sleeping under the bridge does not seem appealing either.

Walking toward the shelter brings back the terrible night's sleep he had the previous week, caused by people snoring and yelling at each other. As he is about to open the door, he sees the staff member at the front desk who he feels treated him unfairly in the past. He walks by the shelter and toward the bridge.

As he walks further down the road, he can feel the cold cutting through his coat already, and the sun is still up. He has not had a chance to shower in a few days, and even the not-so-great showers at the shelter would warm him up. As he approaches the bridge, he sees a couple of people already in the spot he likes because it blocks out a good amount of sound and light from the road above. He hesitates, not knowing what to do.

Avoidance/avoidance is hard for the client and for us. In the above situation, we would want the client to have the safety of the shelter, or even better, have them in a permanent housing situation. However, if we push too hard for the choice, the client will start to feel resistance toward that choice.

The third type of ambivalence is approach/avoidance. In this situation, there is only one choice to consider, and it has both strong positive and negative aspects. When the client moves toward the decision, the negatives become more apparent, but moving away only accentuates the positive. Approach/avoidance is a common type of ambivalence facing our clients (Miller & Rollnick, 2012).

One example of approach/avoidance ambivalence is whether a client should engage in medical care and start treatment for a chronic medical condition such as HIV. HIV medication, like many other treatments, saves lives. Today someone can live a normal and healthy life if they are adherent to their treatment regimen. There are many benefits, including not dying, that result from choosing to engage and follow medical treatment.

If you are not in the HIV field, it would be easy to think that every person who knows they have HIV and who has access to medical care would be getting treatment and medication to save their lives. The Centers for Disease Control and Prevention (CDC, 2017) show that only around 40% of clients who know they are living with HIV are successfully engaged in care and prescribed lifesaving medication. These findings demonstrate the power of the approach/avoidance type of ambivalence.

Digging deeper, we realized that HIV care is much more than just taking a prescribed medication. To achieve the desired medical outcomes, a client must overcome many avoidance factors. Many have fears about others in their community finding out that they have a disease that still carries lots of stigma. If people knew about it, they might lose their friends, family, and even employment.

Clients must engage with a medical provider, despite negative medical experiences in the past where they felt undervalued and dehumanized. Feeling the need to hide their disease leads to elevated levels of shame every time they go to the clinic or take their pill. Even though the medication will save their life, it does have side effects that diminish the quality of life. For a person living an otherwise stable and happy life, these side effects are worth the benefits. For someone struggling with addiction, poverty, stigma, and unhealthy relationships, the pain associated with side effects can push them outside their window of tolerance.

As a client considers engaging in HIV care, there are many powerful reasons to consider this change. As contemplation moves to preparation, anxiety starts to grow, and we can often see the flight-or-freeze response kick in as a reaction to this increased stress. Emotions such as denial and shame mix with negative past experiences in the medical system, leading to a strong avoidance response. Throughout my work in HIV, I know that many case managers can work for years to help clients find the courage and motivation to walk through the doors of an HIV clinic. Often the tipping point is that the client's health starts to worsen as HIV progresses to AIDS, and only when death becomes a real possibility, does the approach becomes powerful enough for the client to engage in care.

The final type of ambivalence is double approach/avoidance. This type is usually the most challenging, and is all too common for many clients struggling with poverty, addiction, and past trauma. Double approach/avoidance has two potential choices, each of which has both positive and negative aspects. Considering one choice makes the negative dimensions of that decision more prominent, while enhancing the positive aspects of the other option. Moving toward the second option, however, makes its negatives more apparent, while making the first choice seem more attractive (Miller & Rollnick, 2012).

There are few perfect interventions for clients. Engaging in services or receiving resources usually requires some change on the client's part. In my training, an extreme example of the double approach/avoidance has emerged that shows its full power.

Many communities now have housing programs that help those

who have experienced homelessness for years get into permanent housing. These programs are getting impressive results for most clients (Einbider & Tull, 2007; Gulcur, Stefancic, Shinn, Tsemberis, & Fischer, 2003); however, people have seen an interesting problem emerge with a considerable number of participants in these programs. When people check in with clients at their new homes, they find that their clients are storing their belongings in the apartment while continuing to sleep in the park or under the bridge.

Here the client has two distinct choices: sleep outside or sleep in their home. From our perspective, the choice is obvious: sleep in a safe, warm, and comfortable home. We would jump right to the action stage and take, what to us, seems like the only logical step. However, many clients are put in these situations before they have had a chance to go through the initial phases of the stages of change. This premature push into the action stage is compounded by the epigenetic reality that their mind and brain have been structured in a way to survive outside on the streets.

This epigenetic expression helped them survive homelessness and it will take time to adjust to the quiet, enclosed, and solitary reality of a single occupancy apartment. While the choice to make the apartment home is compelling on many levels, it also holds many challenges for a brain firmly structured to survive the streets.

Even if the client struggles, having been in a home versus just talking about it as an option offers them a chance to experience the benefits of being permanently housed. If a helper can identify the double approach/avoidance ambivalence, they can work with the client to weigh the two options and talk through the fear of sleeping in a new isolated environment. The helper can also give space for the client to express some of the loss of social connections and life changes that leaving the street requires. For most clients, a little time to focus and process this ambivalence helps them adjust to their new living environment, and the positive aspects of housing help them move quickly through the stages of change.

Ambivalence statements are incredibly powerful. As a reminder, an ambivalence statement puts forth the reason to stay the same (connected with *and*), then the desire, reason, or need to change. "It sounds like you are not ready to give up fast food *and* you are worried about how your high cholesterol and diabetes will affect your future health." Ambivalence statements are complex reflections that help clients to consider and struggle with their own ambivalence.

Now consider your own change:

- *Take a moment to think about your change. Can you come up with an ambivalence statement that reflects your dominant sustain and change talk?*
- *Now think deeper. What type of ambivalence are you struggling with around your change?*

While it matters little to clients which label you put on their ambivalence, it gives you the understanding to guide your reflections and summaries to help the client gain more insight to their struggles. Ambivalence by nature is uncomfortable. It is psychologically difficult to sit with the consequences of your choices and behaviors.

Ambivalence statements are an efficient way to bring about cognitive dissonance. Cognitive dissonance creates motivation for positive behavioral changes. It arises when a client becomes discontented with the status quo and recognizes that there is an unrealized opportunity to improve their situation and live a life more aligned with their values and aspiration. The next step will go into more detail around this concept and show how working from an understanding of ambivalence can help the client find energy for action.

STEP 3: COGNITIVE DISSONANCE

Reflecting ambivalence is a quick and effective way to elicit cognitive dissonance. Evoking clients to discuss their change, discrepancies, and values helps turn the uncomfortable experience of cognitive dissonance into action. Step 3 of mindsight is a powerful step that connects a client's desire, reason, and need to the core of who they are as a person.

Discrepancies are the differences between the client's desired life and their current reality. To help the client see discrepancies, we need to bring values into the conversation. Values are a hierarchy of important concepts or rules that guide the client's thinking and behavior. What the client 'likes' and finds compelling is at the top of the hierarchy, and what the client loathes is at the bottom (Rock, 2009).

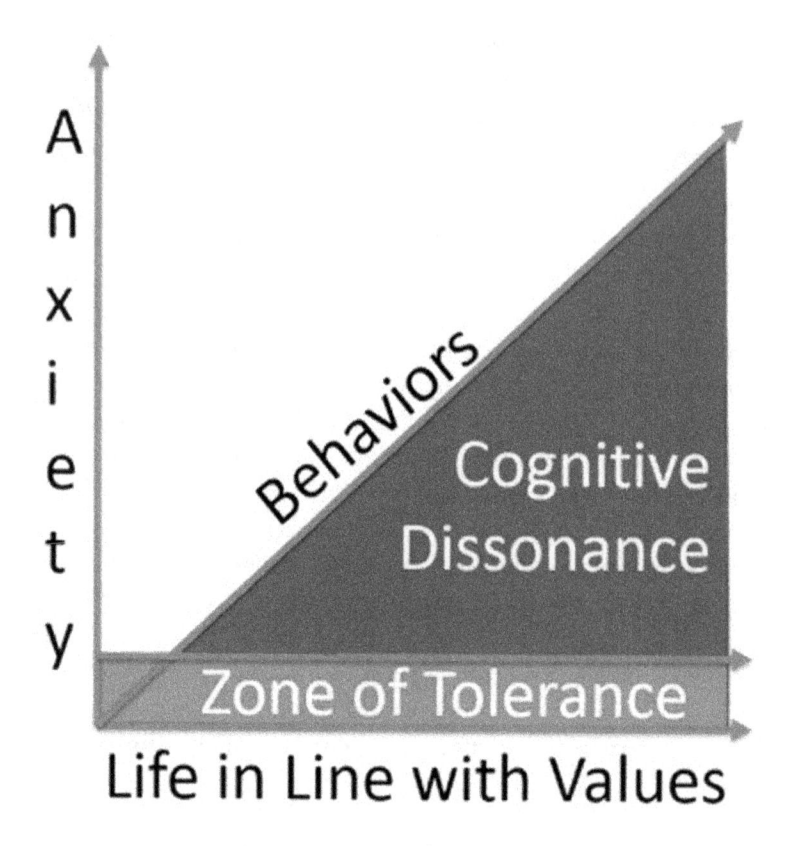

Figure 11-1: Cognitive Dissonance (Miller & Rollnick, 2012).

    This chart will help guide our exploration of mindsight and the relationship between values, behaviors, and cognitive dissonance. The variable on the horizontal axis is the degree to which the client is living a life in line with their values. The vertical axis variable is the amount of anxiety the client is experiencing. The final variable is the client's behavior. As the graph shows, the more a client's behavior is in line with their values, the less anxiety, in the form of cognitive dissonance, they will experience.

    The zone of tolerance describes the degree that behaviors can be out of line with values without causing the client to experience cognitive dissonance. For example, let's say you value your health. You have not eaten well or exercised for several days while on vacation. You promise yourself to eat better once you get home. The night you return, a friend comes over to hear about your trip and brings your favorite dessert and a bottle of wine. Not wanting to be rude, you eat the dessert and help to finish off the bottle. After the friend leaves, you start to feel guilty about not only eating that dessert and drinking the glasses of wine, but also all the unhealthy food you ate on vacation. Cognitive dissonance kicks in; if it is strong enough, you might get up early the next day to get a jog in before work (Miller & Rollnick, 2012).

On the other hand, let's say you have had a healthy week of eating and exercising. You are feeling good about where you are at and the friend comes over with the dessert and wine. While the dessert is not exactly on your diet, you have been a rock star the last few days and plan to eat healthy and exercise tomorrow. Since you are living your values, you can enjoy the dessert without much anxiety, guilt, or cognitive dissonance.

Clients can tolerate some discrepancies, but the further the behavior deviates from their values, the greater the anxiety and cognitive dissonance. Once the client realizes they are out of their zone of tolerance, they begin to look for ways to correct this misalignment. This is often expressed through preparatory change talk, especially desire, reason, and need, and through discussions about the anxiety and cognitive dissonance they are experiencing (Miller & Rollnick, 2012).

Values are often an overlooked aspect of the change process. The more defined the client's values, the more likely they are to realize that their behaviors are out of line with what they value most. A key task in the mindsight process is to assist the client in identifying their values. This establishes a baseline for comparison with their behavior. There are some simple open-ended questions that can facilitate discussions about values. Here are a few examples:

- Tell me what you care most about in life. What matters most to you?
- What would you say are the rules you live by? What do you try to live up to?
- If I were to ask your closest friends to tell me what you live for, what matters most to you, what do you think they would say?

Each of these questions helps the client connect to the values that guide their lives. Clients' values are often connected to values their family held, or those of the client's faith or spiritual beliefs. For most clients, these values existed before their trauma and the resulting negative behaviors they are trying to change. Connecting to this earlier time helps many clients realize that they have strayed outside their zone of tolerance and creates motivation to reclaim the person they once were or aspire to become.

Discussing values puts the brain in a mindset to heighten the experience of cognitive dissonance, maximizing the possibility for motivation and movement to the next stage of change. Strategically creating a mindset to promote a certain outcome is called priming. Priming happens when exposure to a certain stimulus influences a person's reaction to a different stimulus. Let's look at a famous example, the Pepsi Challenge, to understand this concept better.

In the 1970s, Pepsi launched a nationwide blind taste test, where people were given samples of Coke and Pepsi and asked which they preferred. Most results showed that Pepsi was preferred, even by loyal Coke drinkers.

In response, Coke started its own campaign to counteract Pepsi by doing a similar test. The Coke test was not blinded; participants knew which sample was Coke and which was Pepsi before they chose their preference on taste. This time Coke won by a margin in line with its overall market share. Coke's non-blind test primed the brain by introducing the variable of knowing what the participant was about to drink. Knowing someone is drinking Coke changes the results of the taste experience.

Later, MRI scans showed that blind tasting was processed in different parts of the brain than when the participant knew which drink they were tasting. If the person loves Coke and are told they are drinking Coke, the taste experience is processed in both the taste centers of the brain and the reward centers. The blind tasting only activated the taste centers (Gladwell, 2005). This leads to an interesting question: Did those who chose Pepsi in the blind tasting and Coke in the non-blind tasting really like Pepsi or Coke better?

Priming can also be integrated into our work with clients. Our goal is not to manipulate the client; rather, we want to help elicit brain states that promote motivation for the agreed-upon positive change established in our creation of the shared agenda. Let's look at how priming can elicit preparatory change talk.

Discussing values primes the brain in a way that helps the client get in touch with their true self. Being a person with defined values challenges the sense of unworthiness and sets a powerful context in which to examine behaviors. Let's see how you can bring together values priming and the importance ruler.

Think back to the change you identified at the beginning of this chapter; if you can, please grab a piece of paper and a pen.

Take a few minutes to write down your answers to the following questions:

- *Tell me what you care most about in life. What matters most to you?*
- *What would you say are the rules you live by?*

Now think about your change again and answer these two questions:

- *How does your current behavior contradict your values?*
- *How would changing your behavior allow you to better live your values?*

Next let's take a moment to reflect on your preparatory change talk. Please answer the following for each that apply:

- *What desire do you have to make this change?*
- *What reasons can you identify that make this change important?*
- *Why do you need to make this change?*

Now think about your answer to the importance-ruler question:

On a scale of 1 to 10 (1 being not at all important and 10 being extremely important), how important is it for you to change?

Has the number shifted in any way?

The importance ruler combined with your values is a powerful tool for change. Priming the brain by thinking about values elicits a brain state concerned with what the client cares most about in life. This provides a context to talk about behaviors that are out of line with the client's values. It might be easy to say I'm going to do X and not Y; it is much harder to say that I'm going to continue to go against what matters most to me (X) and not choose option Y, even though it better aligns with the rules I try to live my life by every day.

Besides priming for the importance-ruler question, value discussions lead to other important outcomes. First, they give you a greater understanding of the client. Few clients have ever had the opportunity to discuss what matters most in their lives. Instead of focusing on all that is wrong, value discussions help the client connect to what is important to them, which can be a great source of strength. Many find a value question useful at the end of an intake assessment, as a strength-based method to transition from a difficult conversation.

Second, value discussions help build partnership and worth. Asking values questions changes the energy and focus of the conversation, as the client talks about the good that lies within them. It also helps the client separate their problems from themself as a person.

Third, living within one's values can be a powerful goal for treatment or services. For a client in the initial stages of change, thinking about changing behaviors might be too difficult. The same client might be able to talk in detail about what it would mean to live life per the values of their faith or other deeply held beliefs. It might take some time for the client to move from global conversations about values to changing behaviors, but values can provide a critical starting point for eliciting change talk.

Now let's continue our journey into mindsight by looking at the next step, hope and self-efficacy.

STEP 4: HOPE AND SELF-EFFICACY

We have talked a great deal about hope and self-efficacy throughout *Connecting Paradigms*. As part of our discussion on mindsight, I want to add one more practical exercise to build hope and self-efficacy. All clients have a set of strengths that can be positioned to create hope and self-efficacy, but not all clients can see this ability in themselves. This lack of self-efficacy often results in the fixed mindset discussed in the last chapter. This step will provide a strategy to help elicit change talk around the client's ability to change.

Talking about past changes primes the brain to think of one's abilities in a positive light, resulting in increased self-efficacy. Let's look at your change again to introduce a more in-depth process that can facilitate discussions about strengths and the ability to change.

Think about your change again and answer these three questions:

- *What five changes have you made in your life that were difficult for you?*
- *What five personal strengths have you utilized to make these changes in the past?*

- *Given what you know about yourself, how could you make this new change successfully?*

Finally, let's return to the confidence question and answer:

On a scale from 1 to 10 (1 being not at all confident and 10 being extremely confident), how confident are you that you could make this change?

Has your number changed?

Take a moment to reflect on this process. How did thinking about your strengths influence your perception of the change you want to accomplish? This exercise is designed to elicit preparatory change talk about the client's ability to change. Many clients walk through the door with little or no hope or self-efficacy. What little hope they do have for a better life, they often put on your shoulders. Through affirmations and the use of tools like the importance ruler, we can help the client find the strength hidden inside of them.

The other critical aspect of hope in mindsight is helping clients start to visualize a new future. For many clients struggling with trauma and just trying to survive day after day, they might not have thought much about the tangible aspects of what a better future may hold. Things like stable housing, employment, and healthy relationships are difficult to grasp and do not elicit much motivation until they become concrete possibilities.

Energy for motivation comes from cognitive dissonance, but it needs somewhere to go. Helping a client realize that they are not living a life aligned with their values can be harmful if we do not provide pathways to a better future. In the next chapter, we will examine the critical role of planning in helping clients realize their hope for a better future.

STEP 5: MOTIVATION

The last step of mindsight is motivation. Energy for action comes when desire, reason, and need increase enough to move the client from contemplation to preparation and action. Self-efficacy and hope for a better future start to turn hesitation and uncertainty into motivation to realize future possibilities.

Motivation is the energy to act. This energy is not infinite and will fluctuate depending on numerous psychological, social, and environmental factors. Helping clients find motivation can be a long journey in and of itself.

Once motivation is established, we want to continue working on mindfulness and self-efficacy while celebrating and affirming any action toward the change. In the next chapter, we will examine how the role of planning in directing the client's emerging motivation can increase likelihood for success. A strong plan is critical in turning motivation into action toward the life the client desires and deserves.

CHAPTER 12
MI PROCESS PLAN

The last process of MI is to plan. Planning is a collaborative process combining our expertise of resources with the client's knowledge of what works best for their unique situation. In this step, the work of the helper and client becomes more concrete. Together we create a plan of action that provides the client with a direction to maximize motivation and success.

Research into the act of planning has uncovered an important concept called implementation intention. Implementation intention demonstrates that clients are more likely to make a difficult change when they have a specific plan and express their intention to another person to carry it out. Collaboratively creating a plan represents the peak of the MI hill, where preparatory change talk (desire, ability, reason, and need) shifts into mobilizing change talk (commitment, activation, and taking steps).

The MI step of planning can help drive treatment plans, service plans, or other official plans required by our work environments. These plans outline steps needed to help move a client from their present situation into a better future state. Utilizing the concepts in this chapter not only increases successful movement from preparation to action, but it can also bring new life and meaning to paperwork requirements that might seem tedious and often frustrate both the helper and client.

PLANNING AND EXPECTATIONS

From a neurobiological perspective, planning entails setting expectations about a future state of being that is better than the present. David Rock (2009) provides a great starting point for this examination: "An expectation is an unusual construct, as it's not an actual reward, but rather a feeling of a possible reward."

Many clients come to services in a search for a better life. An expectation of a potentially positive result creates a "toward motivation" in the brain. A toward motivation pulls the client to a specific anticipated reward. This toward motivation is communicated through change talk concerning their desire, reason, and need to change. A client might want to stop smoking due to the reward of living a long life and seeing their kids grow up.

Goals and rewards work in tandem in the planning step. Goals are the desired future state, such as quitting smoking, finding permanent housing, or losing 20 pounds. Rewards are the perceived benefits a person might receive as they move toward this future state, such as coughing less, not moving from one hotel to another every few months, or being able to fit into one's old clothes.

The accomplishment of a goal can take months or years. The long-term nature of a goal is why objectives are also important in planning. Objectives are manageable steps along the way to a goal and describe the steps needed to achieve the rewards mentioned above. Even clients with trauma histories and living in high-stress situations can cognitively envision small steps; even if they struggle to see the larger goal, small successes motivate the emotional brain along the way.

As the client makes progress toward the goal, their brain releases dopamine. As mentioned in previous chapters, dopamine brings on a sense of happiness and well-being. It is released when the client either achieves a reward associated with the objective or the possibility of a better future comes into clearer focus. Either way, dopamine elicits a sense of pride and accomplishment, which may be a rare feeling for many clients who struggle with sense-of-worth issues. When someone experiences success, they feel good, and motivation to take the next step on the journey increases. A good plan, and celebrating the successes along the way, creates brain states that turn motivation into action (Heath & Heath, 2010).

ASSESSING READINESS FOR CHANGE

Shifting the conversation to planning changes the nature and flow. It's important for you to know when the client is ready to start creating a road map for change. Miller and Rollnick (2012) have identified several indicators of client readiness to enter the plan process. The first sign of readiness is an increase in preparatory change talk. Increased talk about desire, ability, reason, and need indicates that the client has the motivation and self-efficacy to move into the preparation stage.

The second sign is a noticeable decrease or increase in sustain talk. Decreased sustain talk can indicate a growing desire to take on the challenge, while increased sustain talk can indicate anxiety about taking the first step. You can simply point this observation out to the client and see if they might be interested in exploring some possible steps forward (Miller & Rollnick, 2012).

The third sign is a sense of resignation or passivity, usually caused by the realization of loss associated with making the change. Many of the changes clients face entail giving up something they love, like the high from a drug or the drama of an intense but dysfunctional relationship. The change also involves other unwanted consequences, such as losing friends who are still using the drug the client is trying to give up. Explore signs of resignation by using OARS (open-ended questions/statements, affirmations, reflections, and summaries) and look for the opportunity to introduce planning as a way out of the current state of passivity (Miller & Rollnick, 2012).

The fourth sign is when the client starts testing the waters with small actions toward the larger change. Here, they are taking a quick step over the MI hill. You might start to hear mobilizing change talk for the first time. This change in language might indicate that the client is moving into the preparation stage of change and might be receptive to talking about some next steps (Miller & Rollnick, 2012).

The final sign of readiness involves increased talk about a future state where they have made the change. They may be contemplating the rewards and consequences they might confront in this imagined future. This contemplation often signals that the client is struggling with the last remaining arguments against change. These arguments shift from present ambivalence to future anxiety. You can communicate that it seems the client is thinking a lot about the future and inquire if they are interested in talking about the next steps, which might address probable future consequences of the change.

TRANSITION TO PLANNING

Once you have identified readiness for planning, the next task involves transitioning from discussing the change to constructing an actual plan. This transition is a great time to use a summary statement, bringing various aspects of the conversation together. First, you can ask if it's okay to summarize what you have heard from the client. If the client gives you permission, you can then give a gentle review of the client's change talk. Use the client's words as often as possible and give the client an opportunity to respond to hearing their desire, ability, reason, and need for change summarized in this way (Miller & Rollnick, 2012).

If the client agrees that they are starting to see why the change needs to happen, it creates an opportunity for you to ask a simple open-ended question. Open-ended questions and statements can reinforce the client's autonomy and begin to move toward planning actions: "Do you have any thoughts on next steps?" or "I wonder what you might decide to do."

If the client is ready for planning, the response will probably indicate that they have moved over the MI hill into mobilizing change talk. They might express commitment through a statement like, "I don't know, but I need to do something," or the client might communicate commitment by talking about ideas they have about next steps. It is okay if it seems the client is unready to move forward. It's better for you to return to engaging, focusing, and evoking, than to push the client where they are not ready to go (Miller & Rollnick, 2012).

These questions are designed to provide plenty of room for the client to find their way over the MI hill. Avoid a commitment question, such as: "What are you going to do?" or "So, are you going to do anything about this or not?"

The client will move to preparation when they're ready. Pushing for commitment will bring back sustain talk and might create resistance at this critical moment in the process.

PLANNING AND GOAL SETTING

Next, let's look at some effective ways of integrating goals and objectives into the MI planning process. A goal is a destination where the client and helper want to go. Goals define the hoped-for results and possible futures; they provide direction for actions. Effective goals should also help identify the focus of the helping relationship. This focus helps the client know what to expect and can decrease stress about engaging in services.

Goals are related to the shared agenda discussed in the MI Process Focus chapter. Creating a shared agenda brings together the aspirations of the client, the hopes of the helper, and the direction provided by the setting to create a starting point for conversations concerning change. Concrete goals should come later, when the client is in the preparation stage and ready to discuss a desired future outcome. This timing helps to avoid the engagement trap of premature focus. Shared agendas are useful in setting a general direction for clients in the pre-contemplation or contemplation stage. Goals become effective tools when motivation increases and you are helping the client prepare for action.

When developing goals, be sure that they are straightforward and concrete. Goals do not have to be elaborate. They just need to explain the destination in enough detail so it is apparent to the client when they have completed the goal.

For example, "maintain permanent housing" is an effective goal. However, goals are more effective in MI when they stated in the client's words. The example goal above could be written, "Get a place to live that I can call home," if that's what the client said. Defining exactly what it means to get a place to live can happen in the objectives.

Also, make sure that goals are active and not passive. In other words, a client must do something to accomplish a goal. A way to test out goals is to assess whether a client could achieve a goal if they were in a coma. In a coma, the client could still accomplish a goal like, "Stop fighting with my partner." A better goal would be, "Improve my relationship with my partner."

PLANNING AND OBJECTIVES

If a goal is the destination, objectives are a rough path to get to the destination. Objectives break goals down into manageable steps, which helps to focus both your work and the work of the client. Objectives provide the details of what the client wants to achieve, how they will achieve it, and the time frame for achievement. Next, let's look at some tips for writing objectives.

Each objective should be a small step toward accomplishing a goal. When writing objectives, here are a few guidelines. Each goal should not have too many objectives at any given time. Most people can focus on only one or two things at a time. Too many objectives can be overwhelming, especially for clients who may be dealing with multiple difficult changes.

Objectives should be short-term, achievable tasks. Objectives are a small set of tasks that, ideally, the client can accomplish between now and the next time they meet with you. A formal service or treatment plan might have more objectives than just what the client can achieve between visits. However, you should focus the client's attention on just one or two objectives that they can work toward in a relatively short time frame.

These accomplishments allow for a small celebration at the completion of every objective, which helps release dopamine and increases motivation for further action. Objectives should be active and focus on positive change, not deficits. As with goals, avoid focusing on what they won't do; objectives should describe concrete actions.

The rest of the chapter will examine several types of planning that utilize trauma-informed and harm-reduction approaches while supporting effective MI implementation.

SAFETY PLANNING

As discussed throughout *Connecting Paradigms,* safety is critical to the change process. Safety planning is an effective way to strategically increase the level of safety and reduce harm in a client's life, allowing their brains to focus on their change. Safety plans and the safety-planning process will look different from organization to organization, program to program, even client to client. Some programs do formalized assessments with all clients; others conduct informal safety conversations.

A formal safety plan is an excellent way to structure a conversation concerning safety when working with clients with traumatic histories, mental-health concerns, and substance-use struggles. Safety plans are a strategic way to approach the topic of safety and assess potential dangers. Unfortunately, many only utilize safety plans when a client shares suicidal or homicidal thoughts. A different approach is needed for work with clients with traumatic pasts so that it does not get to the point of them harming themselves or others. Trauma damages a client's sense of safety with self, others, and the world, making reestablishing safety a critical step in the journey toward post-traumatic growth (Stanley & Brown, 2012).

Safety plans work best when they are an integrated part of our work with clients. If a client sees that we care and are concerned about their safety, they often start finding ways to reduce harm in their own lives. If appropriate for the setting and services, intakes, initial assessments, and formal service or treatment plans should include a focus on safety, allowing for, if needed, the establishment of a plan within the first couple of sessions and providing for review on a periodic basis.

Assessing safety does not take a lot of time or effort. The following questions are an excellent starting point, because they give clients the ability to answer at their level of comfort, which often leads to more details and avoids retraumatization concerning sensitive issues such as domestic violence or suicidal thoughts. The first question is, "What would give you a greater sense of safety now in your life?" Often, the client will give a thoughtful answer that helps you position resources to reduce harm and find other ways to promote safety. If the client feels uncomfortable going further, that's okay; just make a note of it and revisit the topic as trust builds.

If the client's trauma history is part of the assessment or discussion, try asking: "What gave you a feeling of safety before the trauma occurred?" This question often elicits an answer that provides insight into successful coping skills utilized in the past. It is much easier to build on these than to introduce a whole new set of competencies. Begin with these questions and, when the client seems comfortable, progress to the more comprehensive safety assessment and safety planning.

When doing more comprehensive safety planning, there are some key topics to evaluate. Feel free to customize these questions to your population and programmatic focus. Regardless of the wording, the safety assessment should answer the following questions:

- What situations/actions put the client in danger?
- What are the warning signs that make the client feel unsafe?
- What coping skills can the client use to self-manage these situations?
- What other people can be contacted to help the client stay safe?
- What are the mental-health resources available to the client?

- What can the client do proactively to improve safety? Examples include removing drugs or weapons, or going to a shelter (Stanley & Brown, 2012; Wright, 2011).

Once you and the client have a shared understanding of possible threats to safety, you want to shift the conversation to possible ways to increase safety in the client's life. Harm reduction is very useful at this stage, as we want to create objectives that reduce harm and not focus on long-term goals that will seem out of reach for many clients. If a client is injecting drugs, they might not be ready to discuss a goal about sobriety. However, they might be open to connecting with a needle-exchange program.

Just because a client has thoughts of suicide does not always mean they are willing to get into mental-health services. Creating some easy action steps, such as calling you, a hotline, or 911; talking to a friend; or going to the emergency room; gives the client alternative actions to take instead of hurting themself. For safety planning, you want to make sure the client has options that are available 24 hours a day and are easy to access.

As with all plans, you should help the client through the creation of goals and objectives. Examples might include: staying at a shelter on cold nights, using clean needles when injecting drugs, using birth control, or talking to a friend when they start feeling depressed. Longer-term goals associated with these objectives might include: signing up for a permanent housing program, engaging in drug treatment, reducing high-risk sexual behaviors, and going to a mental-health professional.

Since safety is such an immediate and urgent issue for you and the client, objectives will take priority over goals. If you do not feel the client is ready to discuss longer-term actions and outcomes, focus on the objectives in your conversation. It does help to write down in your notes what long-term goals you are hoping to accomplish by addressing immediate threats to safety. Even if a client is not ready to discuss the future, having a structured plan for yourself can help guide your conversation and prepare you for potential opportunities for longer-term planning when they occur.

For all safety planning, the most important thing is to never to act in isolation. We can make terrible mistakes when we believe that we alone know what is best for the client. Working with struggling clients exposes us to intense pain and emotional devastation; this exposure can cloud our judgment. If you discover through assessments, planning, or conversations that the client is unsafe or threatening someone else's safety, share this information with a supervisor immediately.

Supervisors or bosses can help process the information to identify actions that need to occur in line with your state laws and can help design a strategy for moving forward with the client. Hearing a client speak of suicidal or homicidal thoughts or plans can be incredibly difficult. Even the most experienced helper should utilize their supervisor or other supports to care for themselves and to ensure the implementation of the best possible strategy.

STRESS-REDUCTION PLANNING

Many clients with a history of trauma need mental-health services to address their past pain and suffering. Unfortunately, not all clients who need these services are ready to engage or have affordable or accessible services in their community. This reality often leaves a non-therapist as the only helper in their life.

It is important, regardless of your role, to help clients alleviate as much stress as possible in their lives. Stress reduction increases the size of the client's window of tolerance, allowing them to address more challenging issues. Here is a systematic process that can help provide the focus needed to eliminate stress, build confidence in their ability to manage stress, and regain control of their life.

1. Fully Understand the Issue

The first step is to identify the cause of the stress overwhelming the client, and to understand the scope and intensity of the matter. Often these are the reasons clients seek services, but presenting problems might just be the tip of the iceberg. The client might say the lack of housing is their cause of stress; however, as you explore the issue further, you might find out that their drug addiction has caused them to get kicked out of past housing programs. Also, both their addiction and lack of stable housing caused them to lose their children to social services.

When you use OARS to explore a cause of stress, you often get a much better understanding of the complexity of the client's stressors. Many of these stressors might include big T and small t traumas as well. Eventually, you and the client will need to find a starting point to begin working on, but having a comprehensive understanding of their problem is where you need to focus initially.

For many clients, this conversation can be the first time the client has considered the source of their stress logically and is not just reacting to it emotionally. Don't solve clients' problems for them. Be empathetic and use OARS to help them fully understand the situation. Taking time to explore the problem and the feeling connected to it will bring potential emotional and resource barriers to the surface, while building trust in the helping relationship

You might spend several sessions at this stage, using the skills presented throughout this book. Once you start noticing readiness for change, ask permission to transition into planning. If you sense resistance, it is just a sign that they are not ready to move on to problem-solving. This reluctance is not a failure on anyone's part; it is the client signaling that they need some more time to process before moving to the preparation stage.

2. Clarify Desired Outcomes

When a client does express a desire to get more concrete, the next step is to define the client's desired outcomes, which can eventually serve as goals for services or treatment. What does the client want to happen in the short and long term? Having clients state their desired outcomes aloud is a way to increase motivation and avoid resistance caused by your stating the outcomes you think they need.

Questions like, "What would you like your life to look like four years from now?" can give you a good sense of how well the client can strategically think about the future. Some clients might outright state, "I just can't think that far ahead." These types of answers or when the client states unrealistic solutions will help you understand that their brain might have trouble grasping abstract ideas like future states.

If they can respond to the question realistically, it gives you a chance to move to the next step of working with goals and objectives. For clients who struggle with visualizing future states, try to calibrate the conversation to their ability to see into the future. This calibration is critical for matching your planning to the neurobiological ability of the client. With practice and small successes, clients will gain the capacity to think further into the future. Your initial goal is to ensure that your communication matches their present ability.

For clients with limited abilities to see into the future, statements like, "Tell me a couple of small things that we could do today to help you _____." The blank might be "feel better," "get a safe place to sleep," "worry less about your children's safety," or "gain confidence to go on a job interview." Bringing the outcome closer to the present keeps the planning conversation going and addresses some of the urgent issues that are preventing the client from seeing further into the future.

3. Create a Plan

Finally, create a simple plan of action. Make sure the plan contains multiple strategies. If only one strategy is created and it does not work, it leaves you and the client with nothing but failure. Creating multiple strategies, the simpler the better for most clients, helps relax the rigid and fixed mindset of clients. It helps them learn to be more flexible. Seeing a setback as something that needs a different approach, instead of seeing an outright failure, helps build resiliency and a growth mindset.

Check in often with the client on their plan. Promote flexibility by adjusting as circumstances change. Most importantly, give the client the best chance to succeed. Going back to the plan and checking off accomplishments can be a huge boost to the client's self-esteem and can build confidence for embracing more challenging tasks.

MOTIVATIONAL INTERVIEWING PLANNING AND TRADITIONAL PLANNING CYCLES

Most helpers utilize a traditional planning cycle in their work. These often take the form of a treatment plan, service plans, or other processes that require setting goals and objectives. Ideally this cycle guides the focus of our work with the client. MI planning strategies can support this work and make it more meaningful.

Unfortunately, many helpers are required to structurally plan from their first contact with the client. Ideally, the flow of the relationship and journey through the stages of change would guide this process. Hopefully, in the future, we will rethink this approach. If planning, and the paperwork it requires, reflects the change and healing journey, we could relax the rigidity, positioning planning as a supportive and positive experience for both client and helper. Until this change occurs, we must do the best we can to use planning to promote engagement and limit the engagement traps of premature focus and labeling.

Traditional planning with a client is a process that happens on a periodic basis. It is a cycle that the helper goes through with clients during their work together. The planning cycle is a process that links care from initial assessment through discharge.

Typically, traditional planning starts with information gathered and an intake that might include formal and informal assessments. This information is utilized to set goals and objectives. These goals and objectives are monitored and updated to ensure appropriate focus and confirm that services and referrals are meeting the changing needs of the client. Monitoring also is supported by notetaking, which documents the client's progress in services. Ideally, discharge happens when the client has completed the goals and objectives derived from the assessment.

Prematurely transiting to planning forces the client to think as if they are in the preparation or action stages. For a client who is in pre-contemplation or contemplation, this can damage the new relationship with the helper and lead to disengagement. The reliance on assessments and intakes, especially those designed to help diagnosis mental illness or addiction, can make the client feel like you are more concerned with finding the right label for them and less interested in getting to know them as a person. This labeling can also lead to disengagement and frustration.

We presented some strategies in the chapters MI Process Engage and MI Process Focus to help counteract these pitfalls. One strategy is to focus early planning on creating a shared agenda, and to put off more structured planning for later. Asking questions such as, "What would you like to get out of our work together?" can provide you with a general direction that can be supported by more formal goals once the client enters the preparation stage.

Utilizing the shared agenda approach also provides you with the opportunity to bring up some of the goals of the program and your general hopes for all your clients. By saying, "One of our program goals here is to help all our clients get permanent housing," or "We aspire for all our students to graduate or get their GEDs before leaving the program," opens the door to larger discussions without forcing commitment.

Some clients might come in ready to work; if they are in the preparation stage, this will become apparent during the shared agenda discussions. If they are ready, there is no reason not to move on to more structured planning. Transition with a statement such as, "It sounds like you are ready to pursue your GED; do you mind if I share some steps with you that have helped many of my clients accomplish this important goal?" A statement like this still gives the client the ability to pull back and say they are not ready. However, most often, this type of statement leads to setting "getting my GED" as the goal, and then setting some smaller objectives needed to guide the action stage.

Remember that clients will be in various stages around specific goals. It is important to keep in mind that a client is never in just one stage of change; instead clients exist in different stages around different changes. They might be in pre-contemplation around getting permanent housing, contemplation concerning their addiction, and action around accessing mental-health services. Keeping this in mind can help you plan effectively and avoid the disengagement pitfalls. Success on one goal can build self-efficacy around more difficult ones.

Planning, done strategically, helps to maximize motivation toward strategic actions that lead to the results both you and the client seek. It also provides concrete accomplishments that can be celebrated, increasing motivation even further. The more fluid planning is, the more effective it will be for clients dealing with a variety of serious issues. As Alan Lakein (1973) stated, "Control begins with Planning. Planning is bringing the future into the present so that you can do something about it now."

CHAPTER 13
POST-TRAUMATIC GROWTH

The goal of trauma-informed services is helping clients achieve post-traumatic growth. Post-traumatic growth is the emergence of a transformed person out of the pain and suffering of trauma. There is a burst of energy and motivation that comes from understanding that if one can live through the hell of their traumatic past, they can start building a new and better life.

Post-traumatic growth takes time, support, and resources, and every client's journey will be unique. Some clients have been under the weight of trauma for decades and it is unrealistic to expect this transformation to happen in six sessions or by only taking a pill. To transform trauma into strength, the client first needs to get back on their feet, which requires shifting their self-concept from that of a victim or a person with little value to the self-concept of a person who has worth and something positive to contribute to other people and their community.

Surviving being knocked down by life is resilience. The ability to gain strength and wisdom from the experience of being knocked down is post-traumatic growth. My clients' level of resiliency has amazed me over the years. It is hard to conceptualize how they continue to face the pain and hardships that many have known their entire lives. While these struggles have taken their toll, these clients find something inside themselves to get up every day and face an existence full of trauma and suffering.

Each client who walks through the door comes in with an incredible amount of resiliency. However, most have not had the opportunity to translate their ability to survive tremendous hardship into the type of wisdom that would help them put their pain behind them and start living a more fulfilled and happier life. Those stuck in survival mode are limited in their ability to utilize their resiliency to realize meaningful change and heal from their trauma.

In this closing chapter, we will build upon the knowledge already present in *Connecting Paradigms* and explore how we can help clients take the final steps in their journeys of change and healing. Aspects of this work lie in the domain of qualified mental-health professionals and the mental-health services they provide. Ideally, all clients would be open and ready to engage in such services. Knowing that this is not always the case, we will explore ways to support post-traumatic growth's emergence in a more general sense. In doing so, I will point out areas I believe should be addressed by a mental-health professional with specialized training in trauma-specific treatment.

RESOURCES

Throughout *Connecting Paradigms*, we have explored the power of the environment and the importance of safety. As a therapist, I was always ready to help clients relieve their pain and suffering, and I had many skills to assist in their process. However, I understood that if my clients had to focus on their basic needs, I needed to address those needs first before moving on to more therapeutic interventions.

Housing, food security, harm reduction around addiction, heat, and medical care will take priority for most clients over mental-health services and addressing past trauma. We should not think of connecting clients to resources that meet basic needs and create safety as separate from the post-traumatic growth journey. Without these variables in place, they probably will not have the focus or energy to take the journey in the first place.

SOCIAL NETWORKS

You're the average of the five people you spend the most time with (Rohn, 2010).

Many clients struggling with homelessness, addiction, poverty, and other difficult social issues find themselves surrounded by people who share the same struggles. There is not anything inherently wrong with this fact; however, the emerging science of social networks demonstrates how emotions and behaviors are contagious, and clients (and everyone for that matter) will mirror the emotions and behaviors of those with whom they spend the most time. For many clients, part of their growth process involves the difficult process of changing the makeup of their social network.

Recent research presented in Christakis and Fowler's (2009) book *Connected: The Surprising Power of Our Social Network* provides the findings behind the effects of social networks on the individual. While the percentage can vary slightly depending on what is measured, there has emerged a strong connection between the characteristics of a person's social network and their behaviors and emotional health. Research shows three levels of influence from social networks. The first level of influence is that of immediate relationships or people with whom you have frequent interactions. The second tier of influence comes from the people who are in relationships with these immediate relationships. Finally, the third level originates from the people in relationships with the people who are in relationships with your immediate relationships (Christakis & Fowler, 2009).

Whether researchers are measuring someone's chances for heart disease, smoking, or happiness, those with whom they regularly interact will increase that person's chances for that characteristic by around 15%. Here is an example to demonstrate the concept. Let's say you have a close friend, Sarah, from college, who has moved to your town. You have kept in touch with Sarah on Facebook and with holiday cards, but haven't spent much time with her since college. When you meet up to reconnect, you find that you and Sarah "click," just like during college. You start seeing Sarah weekly, if not more often, and Sarah becomes an immediate relationship in your network. Based on the research, if Sarah smokes, your chances of smoking will increase by roughly 15%. If Sarah struggles with depression, your risk for depression will also increase. On the other hand, if Sarah loves to take long bike rides on weekends or enjoys regular massages, you increase your chances of picking up these behaviors as well.

Emotions, behaviors, and habits are contagious. Now, this is where the research gets fascinating and maybe a little scary, depending on the social network. While our friends and family influence our behavior by around 15%, researchers also found that people are influenced by the family and friends of our immediate relationships by 10%, and by their friends and family by 7% (Christakis & Fowler, 2009).

In the above example, Sarah's family and friends are influencing you by 10%, even if you have never met them! You might catch the biking bug or a love of sushi from Sarah, but it is likely that Sarah caught it from one of her friends, who was introduced to it by yet another friend. We all live in a web of relationships; these discoveries show the true power of our social networks.

One of the most powerful moments for many client's social networks is when they meet an empathetic and compassionate helper. You start to shift the balance in their network. As powerful as you are, you are only one person, so if all their other relationships are unhealthy, your influence will still be limited (Christakis & Fowler, 2009).

The achievement of post-traumatic growth is often dependent on a client thinking differently about the people in their lives. They need to understand that those around them are influencing them in both positive or negative ways. After presenting an example like the one with Sarah above, you can introduce some simple questions to help them gain insight into the effects of their network.

- What are the top five emotions that you encounter in your normal week?
- What positive behaviors are you exposed to through your interaction with friends and family?
- What negative behaviors are you exposed to through your interaction with friends and family?

With a little knowledge about their social network, the client can come to their own conclusions about the effects of their relationships. This exercise can build mindsight and create desire, reason, or need to rethink their network.

As mentioned previously, other clients might struggle with isolation, which has challenges as well. Whether the client is isolated or interacting with people who promote behaviors contrary to their desired change, there is one relationship shown to promote resiliency. The power of a role model is often critical in many clients' journeys to post-traumatic growth.

ROLE MODELS

As you build trust and safety, clients might be open to connecting with others who can serve as role models for what the client can accomplish, despite their current and past struggles. In their book *Resilience*, Southwick and Charney (2012) state

> *All of the resilient individuals we interviewed have role models whose belief, attitudes and behaviors inspire them.*

They also found that people incorporate aspects of a respected person into their personality. Role models provide templates for success. They do this by demonstrating values, ways of thinking about the world, and successful behaviors that people can emulate in their own lives.

Role models build motivation and courage by connecting the client intellectually and emotionally to someone who has accomplished something they thought might be impossible for them ever to achieve. Many clients will find inspiration in someone who has struggled with the problems they currently face. If you can provide a structured and safe way to connect clients to role models, it can be a crucial step in the client's journey to change and growth (Southwick & Charney, 2012).

Sponsors in Alcoholics Anonymous, peer outreach, educational programs, and mentors such as Big Brothers and Big Sisters all provide role models in structured programs where clients can connect with someone motivated to help them with the next steps of their journey. You should identify appropriate opportunities for clients to connect with those who have overcome or are overcoming their struggles and are in a healthy enough place to give back.

Healthy role model relationships are incredibility beneficial for both parties. Many people who have been through and recovered from traumatic events feel called to give back to those who are experiencing similar struggles. Becoming a role model is a critical final step in many clients' journeys as they use their strength and wisdom to help others.

FACING TRAUMATIC PASTS

The next aspect of post-traumatic growth is the ability of the client to face their traumatic past. Trauma and fear go hand in hand. It is natural for the client to fear anything their mind associates with their traumatic experiences. Fear is an internal reaction to a dangerous stimulus in the environment that pushes the client toward a flight, fight, or freeze response. In many cases, fear is a contributing factor to retraumatization, making the memories of the traumatic experience that much more intense.

Fear can keep clients on the edge of their window of tolerance, resulting in lives characterized by rigid or chaotic thoughts and behaviors. Living in fear is a prison, keeping the client from actions that could lead to success in education, employment, and relationships. For many, the key to this prison of traumatic memories and the fear they produce is confronting the memories themselves (Southwick & Charney, 2012).

The old belief about memories was that once a memory was established into long-term memory, it remained there permanently in its original form. Advancements in neurology are challenging this view. Now we know that intentionally recalling a memory in the right situation destabilizes it for a brief period before it is reconsolidated back into long-term memory (Parnell, 2008).

This destabilization allows clients to reconstruct it before it reestablishes in long-term memory. Reconstructing memories is a complicated process that should only be performed by a trained mental-health professional. It often requires weeks or months of training in mindfulness or other coping skills, as well as the creation of a safe and trusting relationship with the professional.

Once the client establishes some degree of mastery, the mental-health professional gets the client into a relaxed state and then has them recall a traumatic memory. Starting in such a relaxed state and with the support of the mental-health professional, the client, who would normally be retraumatized by the memory, learns to stay within their window of tolerance. Some clients repeat this process many times, weakening the power of the traumatic memory each time until its influence is minimized (Parnell, 2008).

Recalling traumatic memories within the context of a trusting therapeutic relationship gives the client the opportunity to learn to master their intense hyper- or hypoaroused states in a controlled and safe setting. Different forms of trauma-specific treatments approach memory recall in a variety of ways, but all have the goal of taking power away from these memories and returning a sense of control to the client.

A powerful, but sometimes necessary, side effect of this step is the emergence of new traumatic memories. As the client starts to gain control over one set of memories, they might open long-repressed memories. The brain will often repress memories that are too overwhelming for it to handle, and these memories can remain implicit, lying in the unconscious, for many years. Implicit memories still affect the client's thinking, behaviors, and health, but the person cannot readily access the memory of the actual event. As they gain strength in treatment, the brain can release these implicit memories with all the intense emotions, bodily sensations, and images associated with it.

INTEGRATION

As mentioned often throughout *Connecting Paradigms*, trauma can destroy a positive sense of self, relationships, and the world. The goal of integration is to help the client assimilate their traumatic experience into a positive story or narrative with them as the main character. Integration allows the client to rewrite their personal narrative so that trauma is a part of their past. It was once a source of pain and suffering, but is no longer dominating the plot.

Integration often requires the client to answer the question, "Why did this happen to me?" If this question goes unanswered, it's hard to evolve beyond seeing one's self as a victim with little power over the experience. Without a positive and coherent personal narrative, the client has no place to put the traumatic experience, which allows the trauma to control the narrative. When the client can answer the question "Why did this happen to me?", they start to regain control of their narrative and their lives (Foa, Keane, Friedman, & Cohen, 2009).

There are often no easy answers to this question. No one should be raped, molested, or beaten, or have their best friend shot next to them in combat. The key here is to find a meaning for the trauma in the present situation, not in the context of the past. In the past, the person was a victim of the trauma, as anyone who experiences trauma is a victim of another person, event, or natural disease. In the present, they are a survivor.

In the victim mindset, most clients find it easy to blame everything bad on what happened to them. Establishing a survivor mindset, the client takes responsibility for their situation in the present and therefore regains control of their life. Finding meaning does not come easily or quickly, but when the client comes through this struggle, the survivor mentality starts to emerge. The emergence of power where there was once weakness, purpose where there was previously a sense of being lost, and meaning where there was once only pain is a powerful experience for both client and helper.

Once the client answers the question, "Why did this happen to me?", the helper works with them to integrate the *why* into a coherent narrative of self and the world. Finding the *why* puts the trauma in a box, providing a starting and stopping point for the pain and suffering. Integration determines where that box fits in the story of the client and their world. It does not take away the devastation that the trauma caused in the past, but dramatically reduces the power it has in the present and future. When the trauma was writing the narrative, it had power over the client's world. When they take back the pen, the client controls the role trauma plays in their life story going forward.

With the pen in their hand, the client can now also start to redefine their world. For many people up to this point, trauma wrote the narrative of the world as a dangerous and harmful place, with people out to hurt and exploit them. Taking back the pen, the client can balance the pain in the world with the joy and hope that it also holds. The client can also redefine the role others take in their world. The abuser, parents, and past lovers are all characters with flaws and their own pain. For some clients, forgiveness is a part of this step in the journey. The key task here is retaking the ability to define one's world.

Safety is also a critical aspect of personal narrative work. As the client moves from the reactive victim to the empowered survivor, they must deal with the consequences of their past behaviors and missed opportunities. Trauma can steal decades of happiness and opportunities. Part of the narrative is dealing with this loss, which can lead to depression and a sense of mourning for a part of their lives they can't get back. The helper needs to support the emerging person with safety around issues of depression and suicidal thoughts.

Integration is a challenging task. There are no effortless steps in the journey to post-traumatic growth. In facing their past, the client takes power away from their traumatic memories. In integration, they struggle to find meaning and deal with the loss caused by the trauma. Through these processes, the brain is slowly building new structures around an evolving personal narrative. At the same time, the old synapses still exist.

POST-TRAUMATIC GROWTH

The destination of the journey is just a start to a new journey. There is a concept in Zen meditation of "returning to the marketplace." Monks realized that it was relatively easy to practice the calm and equanimity of Zen all day in a hidden cave, but that is not the point. The goal is to return to the world, holding on to the lessons and strengths gained from their meditation. The trauma survivor goes through a similar process. It is one thing to master internal regulation and integration in the therapeutic relationship. It is another to maintain this strength as one re-enters the world of dating, the job market, and the dynamics of one's family.

Relapse into old ways of behavior and thought are part of the journey. The old synapses still exist. The helper and client work together in the post-traumatic growth stage to identify dangers and potential pitfalls in the client's world that can trigger a relapse. The helper assists the client, translating their work in service to the greater world. It is one thing for a client recovering from domestic violence to find a job. It is quite another for them to start dating again. This return to the marketplace will be a lifelong experience of mistakes, learning, and growth. The helper provides an objective perspective on the client's progress, helping them to realize when they are repeating past behaviors and thoughts that might put them in danger.

Wisdom is the combination of knowledge, insight, and judgment. Trauma-informed approaches and trauma-specific treatments focus on building these attributes in the client and helping them to bring this newfound strength into the world. This process is transformative in nature and, as with any journey worth taking, has inherent challenges. There will be detours and pitfalls along the way, but at the end, there is a reward that few things can match.

CONCLUSION

The science, research, and approaches contained in the pages of *Connecting Paradigms* demonstrate the complexity of our work as helpers. If every concept in this book is mastered and implemented with perfection, the act of helping someone live a better life remains, at best, a fluid and unpredictable process of small successes and setbacks. Over the last several years, as I have worked with these paradigms, I have come to appreciate the intensity and intricacies of this work in a whole new light.

This light also shines on those we have called "clients" throughout this book. Our work will never fully be standardized or automated because every client has unique challenges and neurobiology. Each client interaction is a small innovation and creative exercise of compassion, skill implementation, and knowledge application.

Few people outside our professions recognize the complexity of our work and the numerous variables that determine the results that we help our clients achieve. One of the greatest barriers limiting our effectiveness is the fact that the knowledge of trauma, neurobiology, and behavioral change does not inform our community leaders, those who create policies and make funding decisions for our programs. In T. S. Eliot's (1934) poem *Choruses from the Rock,* he puts forth the struggle of our times.

> *When the Stranger says: "What is the meaning of this city? Do you huddle close together because you love each other?" What will you answer? "We all dwell together to make money from each other?" or "This is a community?"*

The nature of trauma is that one person violates the dignity of another, causing severe harm and suffering. Unfortunately, when this occurs, there is an equally, if not greater, harm done by the community's reaction to the victim's pain. Eliot's question of why we come together as communities speaks to the very heart of what it means to be trauma-informed. Do our communities and nations dedicate themselves to healing trauma and fulfilling the call to love one another, or do we perpetuate suffering and pain by prioritizing short-term profits or political agendas over the well-being of people experiencing big T and small t traumas?

Human beings struggle with trauma. We quickly switch from watching an act of mass murder or terrorism to the next news headline, episode of reality TV, or sports event. In doing so, lose the opportunity to gain insight from traumatic experiences affecting our communities and those living among us. It is easier to turn our back on abuse, violence, and poverty than to be present with the vicarious pain these issues cause.

At times, especially when it was important to get "shell-shocked" military personnel back to the business of war, nations have seriously considered trauma. But as soon as the war is over, it no longer is profitable to worry about trauma, even though the soldiers still carry their psychological and biological wounds with them long after the guns have gone silent. We are currently in one of these "shell-shocked' or post-traumatic historical cycles. This time, it is all our responsibilities to ensure we do not let society forget not only the cost of war on our returning veterans, but also the cost of child abuse, sexual assault, domestic violence, homelessness, and poverty that occur daily in our communities.

When trauma occurs, there is a moment that challenges us all. Do we collectively have enough understanding, calmness, and strength to recognize the signs and sit with the fact that these terrors exist in our community? A trauma-informed community takes a breath and mindfully looks at not only what the victim needs, but also what societal issues and past trauma contributed to the abuse, neglect, or criminal act. This mindful response allows both appropriate reactions to the pain of the victim, but also hopefully rehabilitation for the person causing the trauma.

As the rates of incarceration and homelessness of those with traumatic histories demonstrate, if profit is our motivation, we can find it easily in traumatic situations. There is profit in prisons and punishment; from a short-sighted view, it is more profitable to just house "criminals" than to offer opportunities for people to heal their past trauma and address the societal issues contributing to criminal behavior. There is profit in treating the mental and medical symptoms of trauma through medication, but it takes a greater effort to address the societal issues that create the need for the medication in the first place. If we are honest with ourselves, as helpers, we can also get caught up in this mindset. While profits might not be our primary motivation, we can easily just focus on managing the problems and forget to put energy toward solving the causes of the problems that lead people to need our services.

We live in a time where the philosophy is most often profit, not love. A city or nation that is created to maximize profit will damage a significant portion of its population as a means to this end. Tax cuts, senseless drug policies, cutting social programs that work, failing schools, and the skyrocketing imprisonment rates are symptoms of our choice to prioritize profits over love. We have explored the powerful science that shows that crime, poverty, violence, riots, and the inability to succeed in the profit-driven city are not the fault of the person, but a failure of the community.

When you think of all the educators, social workers, therapists of all kind, medical providers, those in the justice system, library staff, and people of faith who are called by their god(s) to serve the suffering, our numbers are significant enough to make meaningful change and create trauma-informed communities. The question is whether we have the strength to take a stand and speak truth to power. The science clearly demonstrates that the behaviors we judge and punish occur not because our clients are evil or criminal, but because something terrible happened to them. We can show how poverty prevents the development of the brain areas needed for success in school, the workplace, and achieving the American Dream. We can show that investment now will yield long-term economic, intellectual, and cultural benefits for decades and centuries to come.

If we respond to pain with empathy, compassion, and love, trauma loses its destructive power and transforms into strength, wisdom, and post-traumatic growth. If trauma is met by judgment, punishment, and fear, the suffering is multiplied, not by the abuser or perpetrator, but by the community. As we conclude, our challenge is to think about how our organizations, faith communities, friends, co-workers, political parties, or schools can promote change in our communities. How do you speak truth to power, speak love to profit?

I will give the final words of Connecting Paradigms to Thich Nhat Hanh, who helped introduce the trauma paradigm in Chapter 1. Thank you so much for taking this journey with me and for the amazing work you do for those in your community.

> *When I was a novice, I could not understand why, if the world is filled with suffering, the Buddha has such a beautiful smile. Why isn't he disturbed by all the suffering? Later I discovered that the Buddha has enough understanding, calm, and strength; that is why the suffering does not overwhelm him. He is able to smile to suffering because he knows how to take care of it and to help transform it. We need to be aware of the suffering, but retain our clarity, calmness, and strength so we can help transform the situation. The ocean of tears cannot drown us if karuna is there. That is why the Buddha's smile is possible.*

You are my Buddha!

Continue your learning and join my blog community: www.connectingparadigms.org

BIBLIOGRAPHY

Achor, S. (2010). *The happiness advantage.* New York: Crown Business.

Ainsworth, M. D., Blehar, M. C., Waters, E., & Wall, S. N. (2015). *Patterns of attachment: A psychological study of the strange situation (Classic edition).* New York: Psychology Press.

Baer, R. A., Smith, G. T., Hopkins, J., Krietemeyer, J., & Toney, L. (2006). Using self-report assessment methods to explore facets of mindfulness. *Assessment, 13*(1), 27–45.

Bale, T. (2015). Epigenetic and transgenerational reprogramming of brain development. *Nature Reviews Neuroscience, 16*, 332–344; doi:10.1038/nrn3818.

Bandura, A (1988). Organizational application of social cognitive theory. *Australian Journal of Management, 13*(2), 275–302.

Bloom, S. L. (2000). Creating sanctuary: Healing from systematic abuses of power. *Therapeutic Communities: The International Journal for Therapeutic and Supportive Organizations 21*(2), 67–91.

Bloom, S. L. (2006). Organizational stress as a barrier to trauma-sensitive change and system transformation. A white paper for National Technical Assistance Center for State Mental Health Planning (NTAC).

Bloom, S. L., & Farragher, B. (2011). *Destroying sanctuary: The crisis in human service delivery systems.* New York: Oxford University Press.

Bloom, S, L., & Farragher, B. (2013). *Restoring sanctuary: A new operating system for trauma-informed systems of care.* New York: Oxford University Press.

Burdick, D. (2013). *Mindfulness skills workbook for clinicians & clients: 111 Tools, techniques, activities, & worksheets.* Eau Claire, WI: PESI Publishing and Media.

Centers for Disease Control and Prevention (2016, April 1). Adverse Childhood Experiences (ACEs). Retrieved from http://www.cdc.gov/violenceprevention/acestudy/

Centers for Disease Control and Prevention (2017, June 9). National Center for HIV/AIDS, Viral Hepatitis, STD, and TB Prevention, Retrieved from http://www.cdc.gov/nchhstp/

Christakis, N. A., & Fowler, J. H. (2009). *Connected: The surprising power of our social networks and how they shape our lives.* New York: Little, Brown and Company.

Cole, S. F., Greenwald O'Brien, J., Gadd, M. G., Ristuccia, J., Wallace, D. L., & Gregory, M. (2009). *Helping traumatized children learn.* Boston: Massachusetts Advocates for Children.

Courtois, C. A., & Ford, J. D. (Eds.). (2009). *Treating complex traumatic stress disorder: An evidence-based guide.* New York: Guilford Press.

Cozolino, L. (2006). The neuroscience of human relationship: Attachment and the developing social brain. New York: W.W. Norton & Company, Inc.

Cozolino, L. (2010). *The neuroscience of psychotherapy: Healing the social brain.* New York: W.W. Norton & Company, Inc.

Davidson, R. J., Kabat-Zinn, J., Schumacher, J., Rosenkranz, M., Muller, D., Santorelli, S. F., Urbanowski, F., Harrington, A., Bonus, K., & Sheridan, J. F. (2003). Alterations in brain and immune function produced by mindfulness meditation. *Psychosomatic Medicine, 65*(4), 564–570.

Dweck, D. S. (2006). Mindset: The new psychology of success. New York: Ballantine Books.

Einbinder, S., & Tull, T. (2007). The Housing First Program for homeless families: Empirical evidence of long-term efficacy to end and prevent family homelessness. Los Angeles: The Seaver Institute.

Eliot, T. S. (1934). *Choruses from "The Rock."* London: Faber & Faber.

Finch, C. E., & Loehlin, J. C. (1998). Environmental influences that may precede fertilization: A first examination of the prezygotic hypothesis from maternal age influences on twins. *Behavioral Genetics, 28*(2), 101.

Foa, E. B., Keane, T. M., Friedman, M. J., & Cohen, J. A. (2009). *Effective treatments for PTSD: Practice guidelines from the International Society for Traumatic Stress Studies* (2nd ed.). New York: Guilford Press.

Gladwell, M. (2005). *Blink: The power of thinking without thinking.* New York: Little, Brown and Company.

Goleman, D. (2006). *Social intelligence: The new science of human relationships.* New York: Bantam Books.

Gulcur, L., Stefancic, A., Shinn, M., Tsemberis, S., & Fischer, S. N. (2003). Housing, hospitalization, and cost outcomes for homeless individuals with psychiatric disabilities participating in continuum of care and housing first programmers. *Journal of Community & Applied Social Psychology, 13*,171–186. doi:10.1002/casp.723. with Psychiatric Disabilities Participating in Continuum of Care and Housing First programs.

Haidt, J. (2006). *The happiness hypothesis: Finding modern truth in ancient wisdom.* New York: Basic Books.

Hanh, T. H. (2006). *Teachings on love.* Berkeley, CA: Parallax Press.

Heath, C., & Heath, D. (2010). *Switch: How to change things when change is hard.* New York: Broadway Books.

Hebb, D. O. (1949). *Organization of behavior: A neuropsychological theory.* New York: Psychology Press.

Herman, J. L. (1997). *Trauma and recovery.* New York: Basic Books.

Hodge, T. (2014). *Trans-generational trauma: Passing it on.* Charleston, SC: CreateSpace Independent Publishing Platform.

Homeostasis. (2017) In *Merriam-Webster's collegiate dictionary* (11th ed.). Retrieved from http://www.merriam-webster.com/dictionary/homeostasis/

Lakein, A. (1973). *How to get control of your time and your life*. New York: New American Library.

Langer, E. J. (2009). Counterclockwise: *Mindful health and the power of possibility*. New York: Random House.

Lewis, G. (2006). *Organizational crisis management: The human factor*. Boca Raton, FL: Auerbach Publications.

Lipsky, L. V. D. & Burk, C. (2009). *Trauma Stewardship: An everyday guide to caring for self while caring for others*. San Francisco: Berrett-Koehler Publishers, Inc.

Lipton, B. H. (2006). *The wisdom of your cells: How your beliefs control your biology*. Louisville, CO: Sounds True, Inc.

Lisle, D. J., & Goldhammer, J (2003). *The pleasure trap:* Mastering the hidden force that undermines health and happiness. Summertown, TN: Healthy Living Publications.

Löwel, S., and Singer, W. (1992). Selection of intrinsic horizontal connections in the visual cortex by correlated neuronal activity. *Science* 255, 209–212.

Marlatt, G. A., Larimer, M. E., & Witkiewitz, K. (Eds.). (2012). *Harm reduction: Pragmatic strategies for managing high-risk behaviors*. New York: Guilford Press.

Maslow, A. H. (1943). A theory of human motivation. *Psychological Review, 50* (4), 370–396. doi:10.1037/h0054346 – via psychclassics.yorku.ca.

Mate, G., & Levine, P. A. (2010). *In the realm of hungry ghost: Close encounters with addiction*. Lyons, CO: The Ergos Institute.

Miller, W. R., & Rollnick, S. (2012). *Motivational interviewing: Helping people change* (3rd ed.). New York: Guilford Press.

Murphy, J. J. (2008). *Solution-focused counseling in schools* (2nd ed.). Alexandria, VA: American Counseling Association. Retrieved from http://counselingoutfitters.com/vistas/vistas08/Murphy.htm

Nakazawa, D. J. (2016). *Childhood disrupted: How your biography becomes your biology, and how you can heal.* New York: Atria Books

Ogden, P., Minton, K., & Pain, C. (2006). *Trauma and the body.* New York: W. W. Norton and Company, Inc.

Oxford English Dictionary. (2017). http://www.oed.com

Parnell, L. (2008). *Tapping in: A step-by-step guide to activating your healing resources through bilateral stimulation.* Boulder, CO: Sounds True, Inc.

Pierce, J. H. (2006). The owner's manual for the brain: Everyday applications from mind-brain research (3rd ed.). Austin, TX: Bard Press.

Prochaska, J. O., DiClemente, C. C., & Norcross, J. C. (1992). In search of how people change: Applications to addictive behaviors. *American Psychology 47,*1102.

Professional Quality of Life Elements Theory and Measurement. (2017). Retrieved from: http://www.proqol.org.

Rock, D. (2009). *Your brain at work: Strategies for overcoming distraction, regaining focus, and working smarter all day long.* New York: HarperCollins.

Restak, R. (2006). *The naked brain: How the emerging neurosociety is changing how we live, work, and love.* New York: Three Rivers Press.

Roe, G. (2005). Harm reduction as paradigm: Is better than bad good enough? *Critical Public Health, 15*(3), 243–250.

Rohn, J. (2010). *The treasure of quotes.* Dallas, TX: SUCCESS Books.

Rudacille, D. (2011, April 18). Maternal stress alters behavior of generations. Spectrum News. Retrieved from http://spectrumnews.org/news/maternal-stress-alters-behavior-of-generations/

Saxe, G. N., Ellis, B. H., & Kaplow, J. B. (2007). *Collaborative treatment of traumatized children and teens.* New York: Guilford Press.

Schwartz, J. D., & Begley, S. (2002). *The mind and the brain: Neuroplasticity and the power of mental force.* New York: HarperCollins.

Shenk, D. (2010). *The genius in all of us.* New York: Doubleday.

Siebert, A. (2005). *The resiliency advantage.* San Francisco: Berrett-Koehler Publishers Inc.

Siegel, D. J. (2007). *The mindful brain.* New York: W. W. Norton & Company, Inc.

Siegel, D. J. (2011). *Mindsight: The new science of personal transformation.* New York: Bantam Books.

Siegel, D. J. (2016). *Mind: A journey to the heart of being human.* New York: W. W. Norton & Company, Inc.

Southwick, S. M., & Charney, D. S. (2012). *Resilience.* New York: Cambridge University Press.

Stanley, B., & Brown, G. K. (2012). Safety planning intervention: A brief intervention to mitigate suicide risk. *Cognitive and Behavioral Practice, 19*(2), 256–264.

United States National Institutes of Health, National Institute on Aging (2017). Retrieved from: https://www.nia.nih.gov/alzheimers/publication/alzheimers-disease-unraveling-mystery/preface

University of Texas Southwestern Medical Center (2010, April 1). New brain nerve cells key to stress resilience. *ScienceDaily.* Retrieved from http://www.sciencedaily.com/releases/2010/03/100331080859.htm

Wagner, R., & Harter, J. K. (2006). *12: The elements of great managing.* New York: Gallup Press.

Wilson, J. P., & Lindy, J. D. (Ed.). (1994). *Countertransference in the treatment of PTSD.* New York: Guilford Press.

Wolynn, M. (2016). *It didn't start with you: How inherited family trauma shapes who we are and how to end the cycle.* New York: Viking.

World Health Organization. (2004). Effectiveness of sterile needle and syringe programming in reducing HIV/AIDS among injecting drug users. Retrieved from http://http://www.who.int/hiv/pub/idu/pubidu/en/

Wright, H. N. (2011). *The complete guide to crisis and trauma counseling: What to do and say when it matters most!* Ventura, CA: Regal.

Yehuda, R., Bierer, L. M., Schmeidler, J., Aferiat, D. H., Breslau, I., & Dolan S. (2000), Low cortisol and risk for PTSD in adult offspring of holocaust survivors. *American Journal of Psychiatry, 157*(8) (August 2000), 1252–1259.

Yehuda, R., Engel, S. M., Brand, S. R., Seckl, J., Marcus, S. M., & Berkowitz, G. S. (2005). Transgenerational effects of posttraumatic stress disorder in babies of mothers exposed to the World Trade Center attacks during pregnancy. *Journal of Clinical Endocrinology & Metabolism, 90*(7) (July 2005), 4115–4118.

Yehuda, R., Daskalakis, N. P., Bierer, L. M., Bader, H. N., Klengel, T., Holsboer, F., & Binder, E.B. (2015). Holocaust exposure induced intergenerational effects on KDBP5 methylation. *Biological Psychiatry, 80*(5), 372–380.

INDEX

A

ACE (Adverse Childhood Experience) Study 6, 17-19
action 36, 37, 40, 44, 49-51, 56, 63, 67, 69, 71-73, 75, 76, 78, 79, 93, 103, 107, 112, 116, 121, 125, 127, 129, 135, 137-141, 144-146, 152, 153, 156, 157, 163-166, 169, 170, 172, 175-177
adaptability 41, 100
addiction 3-5, 11, 12, 16, 26, 52, 56, 61, 63, 65, 68, 74, 103, 124, 129, 133, 155, 173, 176, 177, 179, 194
affirmation 72, 89, 90
affirmations 86, 87, 89-91, 93, 94, 100, 111, 137, 142, 163, 167
affirming 123, 164
ambivalence 58, 59, 70, 78, 79, 93, 139, 151-157, 167
amygdala 34, 39-42, 45-47, 49, 50, 76, 77, 128, 132
anxiety 6, 30, 49, 66, 67, 70, 77, 79, 106, 107, 109, 129, 131, 133, 143, 155, 158, 159, 167
anxious 30, 32, 42, 96-98, 107
assessment 83-86, 91, 100, 111, 117, 162, 171, 176, 191
assessments 83, 84, 147, 170, 171, 173, 176
attunement 32, 33, 129
auditory 39
avoidance 30, 66, 153-156
avoidant 30, 32, 96-98, 107
axon 35, 36

B

behavior 6-8, 10, 12, 13, 21, 23, 24, 30-32, 34, 37, 38, 51, 59, 64, 65, 67, 69, 71-77, 80, 99, 106, 107, 109, 112, 113, 121, 149, 157-159, 161, 180, 186, 189, 193, 195
behavioral 7, 8, 19, 32, 34, 38, 40, 42, 51, 59, 64, 85, 106, 114, 129, 157, 187, 193, 196
behaviors 3, 5, 7, 12, 19, 20, 27, 29-31, 34, 37, 41-45, 47-51, 61-63, 65, 67, 71-75, 77, 93, 101, 112-115, 125, 127-129, 139, 148, 152, 157-162, 172, 179-186, 189, 194, 195
belief 53, 56, 101, 113, 141, 142, 182, 183
boundaries 83, 96-98, 105, 107, 108, 117
brain 5-7, 10, 14, 19-24, 26-29, 32-34, 36-41, 44-49, 51, 59, 61-68, 73-75, 81, 83, 98, 102-104, 107, 111, 115, 124-127, 129-134, 144, 149, 156, 160-162, 166, 174, 184, 185, 189, 191, 192, 195, 196
breathing 45, 50, 126, 134, 135, 152

C

calm 14, 15, 50, 101, 105, 128, 132, 135, 186, 190
calmness 14, 15, 188, 190
cancer 18, 66
capacity 23, 27, 46, 53, 56, 72, 117, 127-129, 134, 152, 174
caregiver 27, 28, 30, 32, 98
chaos 31, 42-44
chaotic 29, 31, 32, 42, 44, 49, 50, 64, 77, 101, 104-107, 183
choice 43, 56, 63, 67, 78, 79, 92, 120, 127, 145, 152-156, 189
choices 7, 12, 56, 121, 125, 127, 128, 152, 155-157
chromosomal 24
chromosomes 35
closed-ended 84, 91, 94
cognitive 8, 14, 19, 27-29, 39, 41, 49, 63, 76, 81, 115, 121, 129, 130, 151, 152, 157-160, 163, 191, 196
coherence 32, 33, 41

coherent 33, 41, 46, 184, 185
commitment 10, 52, 57, 81, 138, 140, 165, 168, 177
compassion 10, 15, 17, 21, 22, 25, 52, 54-57, 61, 86, 97, 100, 105, 113, 114, 117, 130, 187, 189
compassionate 15, 16, 33, 51, 57, 62, 108, 112, 181
confidence-ruler 147
confrontation 51, 148
consciousness 4, 133
consequences 13, 29, 46, 47, 64-66, 69, 79, 101, 106, 107, 109, 114, 115, 130, 132, 139, 143, 149, 157, 167, 185
contemplation 69, 70, 74, 76, 79, 116, 129, 137, 138, 140, 150, 151, 153, 155, 163, 167, 169, 176, 177
control 17, 32, 33, 39, 42, 49, 57, 64, 67, 68, 72, 75, 77, 79, 98, 99, 101, 104, 106, 109, 113-115, 119, 128, 132, 135, 143, 154, 172, 173, 177, 183, 184, 192, 194
cortex 34, 39-41, 45-47, 49, 50, 64, 67, 77, 78, 93, 104, 111, 121, 124, 126, 128, 132, 134, 148, 194
cortisol 40, 43, 49, 98-100, 102, 129, 197
courage 141, 155, 182

D

decisional 149, 150
de-escalation 50
defensiveness 76, 85, 90-92
dendrite 36
dendrites 35, 36
deoxyribonucleic 24
desire 31, 42, 65, 69, 81-83, 116, 118, 129, 137-141, 145-149, 151, 156, 157, 159, 161, 163, 165-168, 174, 181
destabilization 183
dihydrotestosterone 98
disassociating 45
discrepancies 157, 159

disengagement 31, 67, 81, 83, 86, 99, 100, 105-107, 110, 112, 113, 121, 176, 177
disorganization 30
disorientation 49
disoriented 46
dissociate 33
dissociation 29, 49
dissonance 151, 152, 157-160, 163

E

education 3, 6, 8, 14, 17, 20, 24, 77, 81, 98, 183
elicit 59, 66, 84, 87, 101, 105, 118, 119, 122, 123, 139, 141, 145-148, 150, 157, 160, 162, 163
elicit–provide–elicit 118
emotional 4, 13, 14, 18-20, 23, 24, 27-30, 34, 39-41, 46, 47, 49, 50, 53, 63, 64, 66, 67, 70, 76, 79, 81, 89, 90, 98, 104, 109, 111, 116, 122, 126, 128-130, 132, 140, 141, 152, 166, 172, 174, 180
emotionally 24, 111, 122, 174, 182
emotions 21, 28, 30, 37, 40, 41, 43-48, 62, 63, 67, 79, 82, 97, 109, 115, 116, 125, 127-129, 134, 140, 155, 179-181, 184
empathetic 15, 33, 51, 62, 99, 174, 181
empathy 13, 22, 30, 31, 51, 53, 56, 77, 79, 84, 86, 89, 91, 94, 97, 114, 129, 130, 189
empowering 84, 97, 119
endocrinology 197
endorphins 46, 101-103
engage 30, 44, 48, 53, 64, 73, 77, 79-81, 86, 94, 99, 112, 113, 115, 128, 137, 154, 155, 173, 176, 179
engaged 24, 64, 72, 74, 76, 78, 82, 121, 133, 154
engagement 14, 53, 61, 81-83, 85, 86, 95-98, 101, 103, 111, 114-116, 118, 120, 129, 137, 152, 169, 176
engaging 12, 53, 61, 71, 94, 96, 127, 134, 145, 152, 155, 168, 172
epigenetic 25-27, 104, 156, 191

epigenetics 10, 22-27, 39, 62
epinephrine 49, 74, 75
eustress 152
evocation 54, 55, 100
evoke 53, 86, 136, 137
evoking 53, 86, 137, 141, 151, 157, 168
evolution 44, 65
excitatory 36
expectations 31, 51, 56, 70, 81, 83, 84, 96-98, 105, 107-109, 117, 165

F

family 1, 4, 9, 14, 18, 21, 25, 30, 33, 48, 51, 71, 155, 160, 180, 181, 186, 193, 197
father 4, 25
feel 16, 20, 30, 33, 51, 54, 55, 59, 60, 65-67, 77, 78, 83, 84, 86, 87, 90, 92-94, 100, 104-108, 119, 122, 123, 130, 131, 134, 135, 142, 152, 154, 159, 166, 171, 172, 175, 176, 182
feeling 4, 5, 12, 30, 46, 55, 56, 60, 64, 66, 67, 72, 73, 82, 89, 93, 94, 100-103, 106, 122, 132, 134, 140, 144, 145, 155, 159, 166, 171, 172, 174
feelings 28, 30, 37, 40, 44, 66, 67, 71, 72, 88, 99, 101, 102, 104, 122, 126, 127, 134, 135, 140, 142, 143
fertilization 193
fetus 26
fight 44, 45, 49, 77, 109, 183
fight-or-flight 41
fixed-mindset 142
flight 44, 48, 49, 109, 183
focus 4, 5, 11, 20, 52, 53, 57-59, 61, 69, 70, 73, 74, 77, 80, 81, 83-87, 90-94, 96, 100, 104, 105, 110-112, 114, 115, 117, 118, 123, 124, 126, 127, 132, 134-137, 140, 142, 145, 147, 148, 150, 151, 153, 156, 162, 166, 168-176, 179, 186, 189, 195
focusing 20, 53, 57, 72, 81, 85, 86, 91, 111, 116, 118, 123, 125, 126,

162, 168, 170
forgiveness 185
freeze 44, 45, 49, 109, 183

G

genes 23-25, 62
genetic 25, 35, 62
genetics 23, 26, 62, 193
gestation 26
glucose 37
goals 43, 54, 57, 68, 71, 81, 82, 84-86, 111, 114, 116, 117, 123, 135, 146, 166, 168-170, 172, 174-177
growth mindset 141-145, 175
guilt 70, 159

H

habits 37, 38, 56, 61, 63-65, 71-74, 124, 127, 129, 135, 148, 152, 180
harm-reduction 112-115, 117, 121, 170
high-long 40
high-threshold 114
hill 137-141, 145, 147, 153, 165, 167, 168
hippocampus 40, 41, 46, 47, 50, 64, 128
hope 4, 8, 9, 11, 17, 56-58, 66, 68, 81, 82, 89, 96, 97, 99, 101-104, 121, 139, 141, 145, 147, 149, 151, 162, 163, 185
hopelessness 4, 15, 72, 97, 102
hyperarousal 44
hyperaroused 99, 135
hypoarousal 44
hypoaroused 45, 183
hypothalamus 40

I

iceberg 87, 88, 173
immobilizes 55, 67
importance-ruler 146, 147, 161
important 2, 9, 11, 20, 21, 26, 29, 30, 33, 39, 41, 42, 45, 48-51, 58, 64, 69-73, 78, 79, 82, 85, 88, 89, 91-94, 96, 98, 101, 105-108, 111, 115-117, 119-122, 127, 128, 130, 132-134, 137, 140, 143, 144, 146-148, 151, 157, 161, 162, 165, 166, 172, 173, 177, 188
inhale 134, 135
inhibition 31
inhibitory 36
insight 47, 51, 60, 69, 70, 72, 79, 99, 104, 116, 119, 122, 137, 148, 151, 152, 157, 171, 181, 186, 188
integration 10, 33, 147, 184-186
intellectual 23, 27, 28, 39, 49, 141, 189
intellectualize 75
intellectualizing 79
intergenerational 25, 26, 32, 33, 97, 197
internalize 90, 112, 127, 143, 148
introspection 101

J

judgment 12, 20, 25, 54, 127, 134, 145, 173, 186, 189

L

label 14, 16, 85, 102, 117, 128, 135, 143, 157, 176
labeling 83, 85, 86, 90, 100, 111, 128, 129, 176
language 8, 10, 22, 44, 52, 58, 90, 105, 128, 142, 143, 167
leading 6, 13, 30, 36, 40, 45, 113, 121, 155
learning 4, 5, 34, 62, 108, 114, 126, 129, 130, 133, 186, 190
limits 36, 47, 91, 96, 107, 109, 142

low-short 40, 41
low-threshold 114

M

maintenance 71-73, 75
maladaptive 20, 29
manipulative 57
meaning 30, 39, 40, 47, 55, 88, 89, 91, 94, 165, 184, 185, 187
meditate 131
meditation 133, 134, 186, 192
mental-health 11, 26, 46, 51, 85, 97, 129, 133, 134, 170-173, 177, 179, 183
mentor 6, 33
menu-of-options 122
methylation 197
mind 4, 16, 32, 33, 50, 59, 61-64, 67, 68, 74, 75, 79, 86, 92, 110, 111, 115, 121, 122, 125, 126, 128, 131, 133, 134, 156, 177, 182, 196
mindful 125, 126, 130, 133, 134, 151, 188, 194, 196
mindfulness 11, 124-135, 144, 151, 152, 164, 183, 191, 192
mindsight 137, 148, 150-152, 157-159, 162, 163, 181, 196
momentum 69, 129, 138
mother's 26
motivation 10, 40, 52-58, 65, 69, 78-83, 85, 86, 88, 96, 101, 103, 109, 113, 116, 132, 133, 137-141, 143-146, 151, 152, 155, 157, 160, 163-167, 169, 170, 174, 177, 178, 182, 188, 189, 194
motivators 64, 65, 139

N

narrative 27, 39, 127, 184, 185
need 2, 6, 14, 15, 22, 29, 31, 32, 48, 51, 54, 55, 58-60, 67-70, 72, 77, 80, 81, 83-85, 87, 88, 92, 94, 106, 108, 110, 111, 116-118, 121-125, 127, 128, 133, 137-141, 145-149, 151, 155-157, 159, 161, 163, 165-

169, 173, 174, 181, 189, 190
needle-exchange 172
neglect 18, 29, 62, 188
neurobiological 11, 21, 22, 37, 51, 68, 74, 75, 81, 108, 109, 126, 165, 174
neurobiology 6, 7, 9, 10, 19, 22, 25, 34, 45, 47, 52, 53, 62, 64, 81, 106, 124, 125, 128, 129, 132, 133, 135, 187
neurochemicals 36
neurodevelopment 19
neurogenesis 26, 27, 39
neurological 10, 22
neurology 183
neuron 34-37
neuronal 37, 194
neurons 26, 27, 34-37, 39
neuroplasticity 73, 74, 196
neuroscience 10, 73, 191, 192
neurotransmitters 36
Noncoding 24
nonjudgmental 33, 69, 127, 128, 144
nonverbal 94, 123
normalizing 73
numbing 65
nurturing 8, 29, 106, 150

O

OARS 86, 87, 89, 91, 93, 94, 100, 111, 116, 122, 137, 145, 167, 173, 174
objectives 166, 168-170, 172, 174-177
open-ended 86, 91-93, 100, 111, 137, 159, 167, 168
opioid 46
overwhelming 4, 7, 20, 70, 93, 115, 121, 170, 173, 184
oxytocin 100-103

P

parents 18, 24-26, 29, 30, 66, 143, 185
partner 1, 52, 54, 61, 66, 82, 98, 114, 120, 139, 169
perceptions 57
perfectionism 42
perfectionist 78
personality 24, 29, 45, 57, 58, 73, 134, 143, 182
pituitary 40
placebo 101, 102
policies 15, 105, 106, 187, 189
positivity 81, 82
postsynaptic 36
post-traumatic 16, 20, 124, 170, 178, 179, 181, 182, 185, 186, 188, 189
potassium 36
pre-contemplation 69, 70, 74, 76, 116, 137, 138, 140, 150, 169, 176, 177
prefrontal 34, 40, 41, 46, 47, 49, 50, 64, 67, 77, 78, 93, 104, 111, 121, 124, 126, 128, 132, 134, 148
pregnancy 26, 197
preparation 70, 71, 73, 74, 76, 79, 116, 138-141, 151, 155, 163, 165, 167-169, 174, 176, 177
preparatory 137, 138, 140, 141, 145, 146, 159-161, 163, 165, 167
problem-solving 40, 174
proteins 24
pruning 26, 27, 39
punishment 188, 189
punitive 106

Q

questions 20, 22, 79, 83, 84, 86, 87, 91, 93, 94, 100, 103, 109, 111, 120, 122, 123, 145-147, 149, 159, 161, 162, 167, 168, 171, 174, 176,

R

rapport 58, 84
rationalization 76
rationalizing 78, 79
reaction 6, 40, 42, 45, 48, 62, 70, 90, 106, 122, 128, 148, 155, 160, 182, 187
reactive 20, 24, 29, 63, 65, 129, 152, 185
readiness 166, 167, 174
readying 49
realization 71, 72, 129, 167
reason 12, 55, 69, 83, 86, 99, 106, 116, 132, 137-141, 145-149, 151, 156, 157, 159, 163, 165-168, 177, 181
rebellion 76-78
rebellious 77
recalling 51, 183
receptors 36, 46
reconstituting 50
recover 13, 19, 21, 24, 64, 124, 142
re-experiencing 47, 49
reflecting 89, 125, 157
reflections 86-88, 91, 93, 94, 100, 111, 137, 152, 156, 157, 167
reflex 118, 121
reframe 73, 84, 144
regulated 49, 111
regulation 13, 14, 23, 27, 29, 34, 40, 46, 47, 49, 50, 64, 111, 126, 128, 132, 152, 186
reinforce 79, 81, 93, 104, 106, 112, 168
reinforcing 9, 56, 117, 137
relapse 32, 72, 73, 75, 186
relational 21, 30, 31, 62, 63, 96, 97, 99, 104, 107, 108, 125
relaxation 132, 135

release 36, 40, 46, 49, 98, 102, 103, 170, 184
reluctance 30, 76, 77, 174
reoriented 50
repairs 125, 129
resignation 17, 76, 78, 167
resiliency 11, 16, 26, 57, 137, 144, 175, 178, 181, 196
resistance 51, 54, 60, 69, 75-79, 84, 85, 87, 114, 118, 121, 148, 154, 168, 174
resources 4, 7, 16, 29-31, 44, 49, 53, 56, 70, 97, 99, 101, 103, 104, 110-112, 118, 120, 134, 141, 155, 165, 171, 178, 179, 195
restructure 32, 61-63, 68
retraumatization 34, 47-51, 67, 83, 96, 99, 105, 107, 109, 110, 113, 121, 171, 183
re-victimized 49
rigidity 31, 42, 44, 176

S

sadness 6, 63
safe 13, 25, 29, 30, 32-34, 46, 48-50, 96, 105-108, 111, 156, 171, 175, 182, 183
safety 13, 28, 29, 43, 48-50, 56, 58, 80, 83, 95-97, 99, 101, 103-106, 109-111, 115, 117, 121, 137, 154, 170-173, 175, 179, 181, 185, 196
secure 25, 28-31, 33, 96, 101, 104
self-actualization 81
self-care 99
self-confidence 67, 69-72, 75, 78, 81, 93, 141, 142, 145, 146
self-efficacy 58, 77, 78, 81, 89, 139, 141, 145, 146, 151, 162-164, 167, 177
self-fulfilling prophecies 56
self-medicate 65
sensorimotor 39
serotonin 102, 103
shared agenda 53, 85, 94, 109, 111-118, 120, 123, 152, 160, 169, 176,

177
sperm 25
stigma 126, 154, 155
strength-based 58, 82, 162
stress 8, 12, 13, 21, 24, 26, 27, 29, 34, 39-47, 49, 59, 64, 67, 68, 72, 76-78, 92, 108, 109, 111, 116, 129-133, 139, 152, 155, 168, 173, 174, 191-193, 195-197
stressors 173
submissive 32
summaries 78, 86, 87, 91, 93, 94, 100, 111, 137, 152, 157, 167
survival 16, 24, 26, 29, 30, 40, 44, 48, 49, 60, 67, 80, 81, 97, 101, 103, 104, 115, 124, 178
sympathetic 40
synapses 27, 149, 186
synaptic 27, 36, 63, 65, 74, 126, 144

T

templates 10, 28, 30, 31, 83, 96, 97, 104, 107, 108, 182
thalamus 39, 40, 45-47, 50
therapeutic 6, 33, 101, 102, 179, 183, 186, 191
threats 26, 40, 43, 45, 49, 80, 98, 172
trail 37, 38, 74
transference 33, 96-99, 105, 108-110
transform 14-17, 151, 178, 190
transformation 9, 16, 142, 178, 191, 196
transformative 11, 132, 186
trauma 4, 6-34, 39, 43-48, 51, 54, 55, 57, 59, 61-68, 77, 81-83, 96-98, 101, 104-113, 124-130, 135, 142, 143, 155, 160, 163, 166, 170, 171, 173, 178, 179, 182, 184-190, 193-195, 197
trauma-informed 1, 2, 7-12, 14, 15, 17, 20, 53, 54, 84, 95, 104-107, 110, 112, 113, 115, 170, 178, 186, 188, 189, 191
treatment 7, 26, 32, 43, 81, 85, 90, 102, 112-114, 121, 147, 154, 162, 165, 170-172, 174, 175, 179, 184, 196

triggers 36, 49, 73, 77, 105, 110, 128
trust 15, 21, 49, 56-58, 67, 77, 83, 95, 96, 99-104, 109-111, 115, 117, 129, 171, 174, 181

U

uncertainty 79, 102, 139, 163
unconscious 4, 30, 38, 62-65, 75, 93, 98, 99, 125, 184
underactivation 67
unsafe 51, 67, 103, 106, 115, 171, 173
unworthiness 67, 161

V

values 33, 57, 97, 106, 117, 152, 157-163, 182
vesicles 36
visualize 27, 149, 163
voice 55, 59, 74, 76, 102, 118, 144, 150
vulnerability 30, 50

W

well-being 8, 14, 17, 46, 55, 58, 102, 104, 114, 118, 121, 166, 188
wisdom 5, 11, 15, 16, 55, 101, 137, 142, 151, 178, 182, 186, 189, 193, 194
worth 55, 66, 89, 106, 113, 128, 130, 149, 155, 162, 178, 186
worthlessness 17

CPSIA information can be obtained
at www.ICGtesting.com
Printed in the USA
LVHW011727121221
705980LV00013B/1851